Praise for *Raising Thinkers*

An important book about parentir
interesting problems. We can raise a better future if we try.

> ~ Seth Godin, bestselling author of *Purple Cow,*
> *Free Prize Inside, The Dip, Tribes* and *Linchpin*

Raising Thinkers is a thing of beauty. Tremaine du Preez's integrity, authenticity and passion shine through in her brilliant and engaging style. Feeling connected, you happily go along as she takes you on a journey of self discovery from which you emerge having gained so much more than you bargained for. I have explored some of the coaching tips with my 5-year-old twins and I can already see positive changes. In this book I have found a trusted friend whose guidance and wisdom I will be tapping into often.

> ~ Sana Raza Khan, mother and ex-Chief Financial Officer,
> BT Global Services, MENAT

Raising Thinkers is the most original, fresh and entertaining coaching guide available for parents. If you are looking for a pre-packed recipe of parenting success, this is not the book for you. If instead, you are looking for smart, engaging, practical ideas to help your kids develop their own thinking and self-confidence, this is THE book for you.

> ~ Linda Scotti, mother, leadership coach
> and Team Development Facilitator, Google Inc.

How do you future-proof your kids? How do you teach them to think critically about the world? How do future mega-trends affect how you parent? What does 21st-century research in developmental psychology teach us about parenting? In this marvellous, well-researched, beautifully-written book, Tremaine Du Preez gives today's parents the insights and tools they need to succeed in that most precious of tasks – raising children who will flourish.

> ~ Paul Gibbons, father and bestselling author
> of *The Science of Successful Organizational Change*

Raising Thinkers is a refreshing and distinctively compelling look at thinking and behaviour by one of today's most innovative thought leaders. While her focus is on children, her insights apply in many ways to adults as well. Tremaine's impactful examples from around the world, her use of humour, and her thoughtfully direct challenge to parents, education systems and educators everywhere argue convincingly that past assumptions about how to prepare children for life must be changed.

Raising Thinkers is a motivating call to action for parents, families, and educational systems worldwide to lead change now so that today's children are better prepared for tomorrow.

> ~ John A. Davis, father, author and Regional Managing Director,
> Duke Corporate Education, Asia

Tremaine du Preez has written a readable, conversational, personal, human and humorous book that is rigorous in its treatment of up-to-date research and theory about thinking. It is an academic book, skilfully written for non-academics. But it's much more than that.

It convincingly makes the case for the need for today's parents to focus on the development of the 'soft skills' which will enable their children to be successful in the uncertain years to come. And thankfully, it is not a recipe book; instead, it treats its readers as adults and offers many tips and insights to enable them to hone their own parenting skills.

> ~ Dr Alan Beggs, father, former Olympic sports psychologist
> and Founding Director of The Human Dimension

Tremaine du Preez

RAISING THINKERS

Preparing Your Child
For The Journey Of Life

Marshall Cavendish
Editions

Design: Benson Tan

Published by Marshall Cavendish Editions
An imprint of Marshall Cavendish International

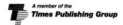
A member of the
Times Publishing Group

Other Marshall Cavendish Offices:
Marshall Cavendish Corporation. 99 White Plains Road, Tarrytown NY 10591-9001, USA • Marshall Cavendish International (Thailand) Co Ltd. 253 Asoke, 12th Flr, Sukhumvit 21 Road, Klongtoey Nua, Wattana, Bangkok 10110, Thailand • Marshall Cavendish (Malaysia) Sdn Bhd, Times Subang, Lot 46, Subang Hi-Tech Industrial Park, Batu Tiga, 40000 Shah Alam, Selangor Darul Ehsan, Malaysia.

Marshall Cavendish is a registered trademark of Times Publishing Limited

National Library Board, Singapore Cataloguing in Publication Data

Name(s): Du Preez, Tremaine
Title: Raising Thinkers : preparing your child for the journey of life / Tremaine du Preez.
Other title(s): Preparing your child for the journey of life
Description: Singapore : Marshall Cavendish International (Asia) Pte Ltd., [2016]
Identifier(s): OCN 956281293 | ISBN 978-981-47-7100-9
Subject(s): LCSH: Early childhood education--Parent participation. | Parenting--Study and teaching. | Thought and thinking--Study and teaching (Elementary). | Critical thinking--Study and teaching (Elementary). | Decision making--Study and teaching (Elementary). | Problem solving.
Classification: DDC 649.98--dc23

Printed in Singapore by JCS Digital Solutions Pte Ltd

For Thane, my wisest teacher

CONTENTS

PART 1

OPERATION PARENTHOOD

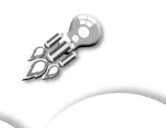

INTRODUCTION

GOING WHERE NO PARENT HAS GONE BEFORE

You will travel far. But we will never leave you.
The richness of our lives shall be yours. All that
I have, all that I've learned, everything I feel...
all this, and more, I bequeath you, my son. You
will make my strength your own, and see my
life through your eyes, as your life will be seen
through mine.

~ Jor-El, Superman's dad, 1978

The desire to understand the origins of our universe is as old as thought itself. We've searched the stars and listened to the darkness beyond for millennia, analysed the celestial crumbs that fall to Earth and pioneered technologies to help us extract the smallest facts from the grandest theories. In the late 1970s a team of European scientists dreamed of journeying through both space and time to land a probe on a speeding comet to find an answer to this oldest of riddles. It was a whimsical idea at a time when mankind hadn't even seen a comet up close. But their outlandish notion grew and grew with complete disregard for the confines of reality until there was no stopping it. It gathered 250 scientists from 11 countries and $1.7 billion of funding for a 30-year journey back to the beginning of the beginning.

Christened the Rosetta Mission, the most conceptually and technologically audacious act of discovery ever undertaken: to chase a comet across the galaxy for 10 years with a probe the size of an SUV ricocheting across our inner solar system at speeds of 66,000 kilometres per hour through megalithic asteroid belts, ice, gas, dust and whatever else is out there. After 19 years of research, committees, permissions and setbacks, it was done. The Rosetta probe was launched in 2004 on an unknowable journey that would, hopefully, last a full decade.

For three years of that journey Rosetta slept in deep space hibernation, alone in a faraway orbit, in the coldest regions of space, 520 million kilometres from home. Then in 2011, she woke herself up and figured out where she was in space by comparing what she saw with stellar images stored in her databank. After hours of searching she finally found Earth and called home, "Hello it's Rosetta. I'm fine, I've just woken up and here I am." Mission control in Germany couldn't have been happier or more proud.

In November 2014, Rosetta reached her target, her raison d'être, in the outer reaches of our solar system – an ice and dust ball a mere four kilometres wide, tearing through space 130 times faster than the top speed of a Boeing A380. Rosetta released her Philae lander to rendezvous with this icy comet known as 67P, and the real work of looking back 4,600 million years to figure out how our solar system developed from ancient primordial chaos began.

Were there risks to this operation? Could the team at mission control have done everything possible to ensure that the mission, their reputations and taxpayers' money weren't compromised in any way? Yes, of course there were both known and unknown risks – all of them huge. Despite 19 years of planning and research the team could never have guaranteed the success of this mission. In fact, when Rosetta's lander reached the surface of the comet, it was greeted with ice and dust far softer than expected. It drifted, bounced twice, failed to fire its harpoons and came to rest in a dark, shadowy crater, well hidden from sunlight. With its last ounce of solar power, it radioed home to say that it was out of energy and shutting down till it found the sun again, or the sun found it.

Parenting today is not too different from running a space exploration programme. As far as funding goes, kids and space bots usually cost more than we budgeted for. The first 18 years, maybe more, are a flurry of designing, learning, testing, correcting and improving the skills and personalities of our offspring. Despite preparing them for the journey of life with the utmost care and attention, there are simply too many known and unknown variables at play for us to be confident that nothing will go wrong. Come launch day we still won't know exactly what lies out there on their paths. The unknown is risky business and exactly why NASA, the ESA and their global peers employ a team of the smartest brains with specialist skills in every area needed for each project. To quote from their website: "It takes hundreds of people; machinists, engineers, scientists, programmers and many others to get a spacecraft from the planning stages to its destination in outer space." The Rosetta Mission took over 1,000 brains to get to launch and even then, success was merely one of the possible outcomes.

Can you imagine the parenting equivalent? Beginning with fertility specialists, a maternity team consisting of prenatal yoga instructor, nutritionist, nursery decorator, financial planner and second-hand car dealer; followed by the prelaunch team of early childhood specialists, paediatricians, fitness trainers, life coaches, caregivers, babysitters, party entertainers – and we haven't even started on school and extra-everything class specialists.

If you are a parent, you don't have to imagine any of this – except the government-funding bit. You will already know that it takes hundreds of specialists, project-managed by you, to launch a child on the path to his or her dream. But there is something that the teams at NASA and the ESA do very differently to you and I, something that helps ensure that all those tax dollars result in valuable outcomes to their space programmes despite daunting odds. Before any space agency launches a space bot off into what seems like unchartered territory, the team will already have spent a great deal of time and resources researching and understanding the environment that the bot is most likely to encounter throughout its cosmic adventure. This includes the stresses that its software, hardware and structure will face over time. Materials are selected that can withstand harsh and unpredictable conditions. Failsafes are encoded into software to maintain contact through a range of projected environments and situations. This is all done to give the space bot the best chance of successfully completing its mission. Even then, success cannot be guaranteed.

The children in our care are being prepared for a life filled with wonders and challenges that we haven't yet thought possible in a future that will look very different from our past. Most of us were raised in a world where there was only one TV in the house and the phone was either in the hallway or the kitchen attached to the wall with a dangling, twisted cord. Madonna was cool. Mom and Dad wielded parenting skills they had gained over the previous two decades. They didn't have Google in their pockets to answer our endless questions, but we still thought they were the smartest people on the planet. Now we are the parents raising our children with unparalleled access to knowledge and resources. Thanks to the Internet we have answers to all of their questions, except maybe the God- or multiverse-related ones. For the first few years, we are the smartest people in the world to our children. After that they go straight to Professor Google and a panel of known and unknown peers.

Our generation found answers in the library or from magazines or teachers, parents and friends. Our friends were children we grew up with, whose parents knew our parents. We were all part of the same community, for better or worse. The environment that will shape our children is less tangible, harder to define and influence and more complex and interconnected than ours could ever have been. The nature of a "friend" or trusted resource has also changed dramatically as virtual friends acquire the same status as the flesh-and-blood kind.

We are going where no parent has gone before. I know that I don't have all the answers to my son's questions and I don't know how to make all his really big dreams come true. But I do have an idea of where to start.

A note about what this book isn't

This is not a book about being a good parent. I will assume that you are already the best parent you can be. I will also assume that your relationship with your child allows you to influence their life. That the basics are covered and your children are fed a balanced diet and clothed in Baby Gap (just kidding), kept safe in the care of qualified carers and, most importantly, loved as much as you could possibly love another human being. We cannot work together on their higher-order thinking skills if their home base isn't secure.

And other assumptions I make

Families come in all different shapes, sizes and flavours: one mom and one dad, a single parent, two dads or two moms or any combination of these. Children are raised in homes with one, two or no working parents, with siblings or none. They are boys or girls, homosexual, bisexual or heterosexual sporting a variety of languages, races, religions and nationalities. I will refer to your child or children as *him* or *her* interchangeably and the family as any variation of the above. *Parents* will refer to a child's primary caregiver or givers, related by birth, law or not at all.

We live in a diverse external world, but our internal worlds, drivers and cognitive motivations are astonishingly similar. That is why this book is written for boys and girls, moms, dads and caregivers from Kent to Kansas, Kenya to Korea and every stop in-between. It does not however, cover the complex cognitive worlds of special-needs children.

1.1

SCOPING THE JOURNEY OF A LIFETIME

Any voyage, especially one where the stakes are high and the destination is unchartered, must start with an objective. Only when we know what the purpose of *Operation Parenthood* is, can we scope the mission. Do you, parent of (insert your child's name here), have a very clear idea of the outcomes that you would like for your child? I'm not talking about whether you want little Xander to be a lawyer like his daddy or Anushree a microbiologist. No, what is your mission objective for their lives? Independence? Resilience? Bravery to go after their dreams or fulfil their potential despite limited opportunities? If you don't know what gifts you want to impart to them throughout their childhood, then whatever the school system serves up on either side of their cafeteria lunches will have to be good enough, won't it?

I asked parents from around the world what they wished for their children and here are some of the answers I received.

"That they grow up identifying their unique talents, skills, values and passions and choose to follow that in all areas."

Jaime, Australia

"To be happy, kind, respectful, balanced and self- assured."

Maxine, South Africa

"To find confidence, love, commitment."

Kelly, Indonesia

"Happiness, flow and resilience."

Menakshi, India

"That they find something in life which they really enjoy and have a passion for. And don't fill up with fear."

Antonia, Buenos Aires

"To be brave and follow their dreams no matter what."

Karl, Canada

I used to wonder how *I* would answer this question. In fact, I thought about it a lot. What did I want most of all for my son? Was it as simple as happiness or fulfilment or some other even less tangible quality? If so, how would I give him that? As with most mental conundrums, the answer came to me when I wasn't thinking about it, on a holiday in South Africa just after my son's 8th birthday.

We spent a morning with a falconer along the aptly named Garden Route in the South. A mesmerising, befreckled, red-bearded old man who rehabilitates birds of prey that have been hurt or fallen on hard times, so to speak. Many of their species balance on the brink of extinction with no government protection or funding to raise awareness of their plight. These birds are his all-consuming passion and love of his life. A life that is entirely funded by donations from the public. Is he doing a worthwhile job? Yes. Is he happy? Absolutely. But would I like my son to grow up doing something he loves that is entirely reliant on fickle hand-outs from tourists over a few summer months? Even if it makes him happy? Hmm.

Then I realised that it wasn't happiness or resilience or even finding purpose that I truly wanted to gift him.

What I wanted most of all for my son was for him to learn to make the best possible decisions that he could. Be a good thinker and deliberately curate everything on the path leading to his future, not simply following the capricious current of life. Besides, my husband and I knew that the decisions we had made in the past had created our current reality, and the decisions that we made today would create our future. My son's life would also be guided and determined by the choices he made along the way. Would that make him happy? We hoped so. We hoped that being able to make good decisions about how to spend his time, what to study, what to read, what not to eat or drink and how to respond to challenging situations in the playground, the campus or the office would make his life a little easier, and maybe, a little happier. The rest would be up to him. And if he chose to be a dreadlocked-bohemian-surfer dude, then at least it would have been a well-considered decision. I hope.

But how could we teach him to make good decisions? Did we even need to? Surely his school would teach him to be a good thinker? We soon found out that, even though school subjects were now considerably cooler than in our day, teaching students *what* to think is still their primary goal. Facts and data are easier to teach and test for. Are primary school teachers even familiar with decision science and critical thinking? Should they be? But were we in a position to teach him how to make good choices ourselves? We'd racked up a fair amount of lousy decisions between us in the past. So lecturing him in the art of decision science, or anything for that matter, would likely backfire before he hit puberty.

What we *could* do was learn as much as possible about making good decisions, thinking about thinking and processing information soundly. Then, and only then, could we coach him. In fact, this is how I came to do what I do as a coach and lecturer in critical thinking and decision making. It was all for my most precious little one – because I realised that I couldn't raise a critical thinker if I wasn't one myself.

Yes, I know, not everyone can devote a decade to thinking and writing about thinking (it's been as cerebral and romantic as it sounds), which is why I have written *Raising Thinkers* as a guide to help you lay some solid cognitive foundations to set your children up for their journey of a lifetime.

So, mission architect, what was it that you wanted for your children? Write down your thoughts here, right now, so that you don't forget. If you are reading an ebook, grab a pen and paper because you'll need them again soon.

_____

_____

_____

_____

_____

As a behavioural economist and lecturer in critical thinking there is zero chance of me forecasting a future based on historical data – my crystal ball doesn't work *that* well. Such predictions would come with a loud thumb-sucking sound and be as pointless as trying to call interest rates in the year 2025 (apologies to anyone who has). But this creates a conundrum for us – how can we understand the forces that will shape our children's future environment and challenges with only historical and current data to work with? Couldn't we rather just sit back and wash our hands of the whole future affair? Leave it to our child's teachers/peers/latest YouTube idol to take care of till she turns 18 and we can tuck her into an escape pod and send her on her way?

This worked out all right for Superman's parents back on planet Krypton. They didn't have 18 years to prepare their son for launch but they did the best they could with what they had. Just before the destruction of their entire planet, they snuggled their new born babe, Kal-El, into a nifty life-support capsule, set his path for Earth and hoped that he would land in loving arms. Wasn't it lucky that he landed in a field, on a farm in a developed country where an elderly, kind and childless couple found him and raised him to be a caring citizen and indestructible superhero, capable only of exercising his powers for good? But what if he had landed in Syria, Siberia or the Congo? He would have needed a different set of skills to navigate his way to superhero status and global stardom. Could his parents even have imagined such a setting for his formative years? How are we supposed to prepare our greatest and most precious investment, our children, for a future that we can't imagine?

By focusing on their journey, not the final destination, because their journey will create their destination.

To do this we can start with current information just like the teams at NASA. Gather information and insights that will help us anticipate a most likely range of environments and conditions that our children will encounter along their way. This will also allow us to model a series of obstacles they are most likely to face and equip them with the skills needed not just to overcome challenges but to thrive in a new, unknown world.

So let's explore some fundamental features of the futures that we'll be jettisoning our little darlings into. The skills that they will need in these settings and what can reasonably be expected from education systems across the East and West. We also ask what can reasonably be expected from us, the engineers of their future selves, given our mental frames and abilities.

I'll end each chapter with a note on its key takeaways and thinking points. Hang on to these, they'll be useful as your children grow and your parenting tactics evolve.

TIPS AND TAKEAWAYS FROM CHAPTER 1

1. What is the objective of *Operation Parenthood* for you? We all want different things for our children. Have you thought about the talents you would like to gift them throughout their childhood?

2. We can't know the future that we are launching our children into, nor the jobs that will occupy them throughout their lives, but we can learn as much as possible about the trends likely to impact their journey through time and help them make informed choices about their future.

2.1

A GRADUATE-RICH, SKILLS-POOR FUTURE?

> Of the many buzzwords making the rounds in Davos this year, "skills gap" is the most ubiquitous. While there seems to be a broad consensus on what the causes of the said gap are – outdated teaching methods and course syllabi, and lack of in-work training – there is less agreement on what needs to be done, or who should be doing it.
>
> ~ **BBC News, reporting from Davos,**
> **World Economic Forum, January 2015**

Did you ever want to be an astronaut? To take small steps and giant leaps across the face of a planet never touched by toes before? To explore the outer reaches of human curiosity in our celestial backyard? If so, the end of NASA's Space Shuttle Program in 2011 would have been a sad day for you and daydreamers everywhere. The end of an era. Sure, it's cheaper and easier to send a probe into orbit than a high maintenance human with a short shelf life, but we're not going to let the machines have all the fun, are we? Rather than being the death knell for manned space travel, NASA's loss created opportunities for smaller, hungrier, more innovative players to compete for the billions of dollars of funding available for the best ideas. Interstellar travel, space tourism and a colony on Mars are all cautiously stepping out of sci-fi blockbusters and onto reality TV. Thank goodness manned space exploration hasn't gone the way of the tooth fairy – our children can still safely dream of donning 3D printed space suits and radioing ground control, "Houston, we're getting there." The UK's National Space Academy is hoping that our children will do more than just dream about what waits at the very edge of our understanding of the universe.

The space industry is a rapidly growing sector in the UK, earmarked to be worth £30 billion by 2030. But it is faced with a perplexing dilemma right now in a country with a record number of students enrolled in university degree programmes – it can't find the right people for the job. The recruiters at the National Space Academy are coming up empty-handed in their search for the right expertise among students with traditional university educations. But they're a tenacious lot at the NSA. Unlike many other industries who look to governments and universities to bridge the chasm between skills produced and skills required, they've rolled up their sleeves and solved their own problem.

With the help of traditional education providers, they have created a first degree-level apprenticeship – the higher apprenticeship in space engineering[1] – to attract more scientists and engineers into the industry's HR pipeline. What Matt Smith's

1   Loughborough College, Loughborough

Dr Who did for bow ties, a chronic talent mismatch is doing for on-the-job training. Apprenticeships are cool again. It's a small beginning but has the potential to shake up traditional, and immensely popular, one-size-fits all undergraduate programmes, particularly in specialist areas. Mark Eighteen is the commercial director of Activate Enterprise,[2] a business working with companies to directly address the skills shortage they face by training new recruits specifically for them and managing their apprenticeship programmes. It's no surprise that they are based in Oxford, in the heart of the UK's tech hub. It's also no surprise that they are very, very busy and will get busier when the UK's Apprenticeship levy comes into force in 2017. At the time of chatting to him, they had 150 vacancies for young people on their books but, "Finding the right calibre of job-ready young people is a real challenge for us." Research that they conducted along with Find A Future/ Worldskills UK, the company behind the UK's largest skills and careers event, The Skills Show, helps us understand why. There is a striking mismatch between what employers expect schools and colleges to equip young people with and what those same young people think they need to enter the workforce. The highest priority for employers surveyed was personal skills for employability, which they cited as communication, problem solving, team work and time management. These skills were stone last on the wish list of school leavers and college graduates. The latter cited work experience as their top priority followed by career advice and interview skills.

One hundred and fifty vacancies is hardly a crisis but if we broaden our frame a little bit we'll see how it is part of an acute

2   www.activate-enterprise.co.uk

talent shortage that continues to grow despite developed economies drowning in graduates. Let's dash around the globe and have a quick look at the state of graduate employment across the East/West divide where we find more similarities than differences.

We'll start with the East, merely because it wakes up first. In highly developed South Korea, the number of economically inactive graduates passed three million[3] for the first time in 2014, a number that is expected to grow in a country with one of the highest university participation rates. In Singapore, graduate unemployment remains stubbornly above average unemployment.[4] In China, advancing to a postgraduate education is more likely to leave one jobless than stopping at a graduate degree. India's well-educated woes are just as economically painful with one in three graduates (up to age 29) remaining unemployed. Craig Jeffrey, Professor of Development Geography at Oxford University paints this in numbers when he observes that up to 27,000 applicants apply for a single state job vacancy in India. What has the current state of unemployment got to do with your child's future? You've probably worked that out by now but if you haven't I'll tell you: everything.

Despite this growing pool of potential, throughout the region employers are struggling to meet hiring quotas. Especially in India, where 61% of employers surveyed said talent shortages prevented them from hiring people with the needed skills.[5] This number rises to a staggering 85% in Japan which boasts a 25% of GDP per capita spending on tertiary education. It would seem that today's unemployed are better educated and less employable than in any

---

3   Sharma, Y. (2014, February 14). Rising unemployment – are there too many graduates? *University World News*, Global Edition, Issue 307.
4   Ibid.
5   2013 Talent Shortage Survey by ManpowerGroup, a US-based human resources multinational firm that surveyed 8,600 employers in Asia and the Pacific.

previous generation. So what is creating this frictional labour market? The World Bank points to a skills shortage rather than an oversupply of graduates. Skills shortage? How is that possible when universities are producing graduates faster than *American Idol* is spawning starlets? It seems that the skills universities are selling aren't exactly what the corporate world is buying. So it's a skills mismatch rather than an outright shortage. A talent gap.

A McKinsey & Company study[6] into this conundrum tells us what you might already suspect: that employers, education providers and young people operate in parallel universes. There is a struggle between fulfilling the oldest and highest ideal of education – to provide good citizens with a strong moral and academic foundation – and more recent requirements of producing corporate employees or entrepreneurs capable of generating profit for stakeholders and, ultimately, sustained economic growth for the country that appreciates their skills most. If you were hoping that this is an isolated issue in the countries I've already mentioned, you'd be disappointed to know that it's not, it's a global migraine. The study goes on to tell us that in Europe, 74% of education providers are confident that their graduates are prepared for work, but only 38% of youth and 35% of employers agree. We can also agree that these different players don't talk to one another and don't understand one another's expectations and needs. In fact, only German and UK employers were able to report that they communicate with education providers.

And what are these special skills that recent graduates seem to be terribly short of?

---

6   McKinsey & Company. (2014). *Education to employment: getting Europe's youth into work.* Retrieved from www.mckinsey.com/industries/social-sector/our-insights/converting-education-to-employment-in-europe

Soft skills such as spoken communication, teamwork, creativity and work ethic. Bet you didn't see that coming!

Despite ongoing dialogue with education providers, the UK corporate sector still feels unheard and is driving research of their own into what the skills gap really means on the ground, in terms of pounds and pennies. What they found is that employers in the UK have put an £88 billion[7] economic value on the lack of soft skills amongst recruits – skills such as initiative, communication, decision making and teamwork. The UK's Development Economics research group says the lack of these skills could significantly limit the job opportunities of more than half a million UK workers by 2020, which is only a few short years away.

In the US, things don't look too different with a graduate underemployment rate of 44%.[8] Fortunately, the debate around this is louder and clearer in Washington than in most other capitals. At a business roundtable with President Obama, Rex Tillerson, a straight talking Texan and chairman and CEO of Exxon Mobil, points out rather adroitly, "I'm not sure if public schools understand that we're their customer. Businesses have a vested interest in the education attainment of potential workers. Failure in the education arena is akin to turning out defective products, and those products are human beings."[9] Ouch, that's harsh, but he's a man with an eye on the bottom line, and a finger on the pulse of the future with a good idea of what skills are needed to fill Exxon's talent pipeline to remain competitive.

Still in the US, Deloitte urges employers to look out for "hyper-

7   The Development Economics research group calculates that soft skills are worth £88bn per year, particularly in businesses that rely on "face-to-face human interaction". Information retrieved from www.bbc.com/news/education-30802474

8   Nawaguna, E. (2014, June 1). *Jobs become more elusive for recent U.S. college grads.* Retrieved from www.reuters.com

9   Peralta, K. (2014, December 3). *CEOs say skills gap is problematic.* US News. Retrieved from www.usnews.com/news/articles/2014/12/03/ceos-say-skills-gap-is-problematic

skilled workers"[10] who possess traits that indicate adaptability, such as creativity, problem-solving and critical-thinking skills to meet future needs. Hyper-skilled? Shouldn't these be basic skills?

Given that over half[11] of large US companies report a shortage in graduates with STEM (science, technology, engineering and maths) skills, it would seem that problem solving and critical thinking are indeed luxuries. I know I'm painting a glum picture of the world ahead for your children. Indeed, I found this research a bit like trying to decipher a Salvador Dali painting from inside the painting. There are things that intrigue me and bother me at the same time, such as why do US policy makers feel that STEM skills alone will solve their skills gap when technical skills are only half the problem? Why does the skills gap even exist and what does it mean for me as a parent? Can I carry on raising my son as usual, believing that he's somehow different and will have no problem finding a market for whatever skills he develops at school and university?

After months of researching these questions I found both bad and good news. You'll have the good first? Perfect.

By 2020, employers worldwide could face a shortage of 85 million high- and medium- skilled workers.[12] That's 85 million vacancies that the current generation of students could access if they have the right training. The bad news is that universities move more slowly than commerce and so are either still oblivious to or playing catch up with the requirements of the corporate world. Fortunately, in most countries across Asia and the developed

---

10 Deloitte University Press. (2014). *Help wanted: American manufacturing competitiveness and the looming skills gap.* Retrieved from dupress.com/articles/manufacturing-skills-gap-america/
11 Rothwel, J. (2014, July 1). *Still searching: job vacancies and STEM skills.* Metropolitan Policy Program at Brookings. Retrieved from www.brookings.edu/interactives/still-searching-job-vacancies-and-stem-skills/
12 McKinsey Global Institute, Washington. Retrieved from www.mckinsey.com/insights/mgi.aspx

West, higher education is now squarely on the economic growth agenda. According to UNESCO, it's no longer an issue exclusive to ministries of education, it's now also on the forefront of the agenda of ministries[13] of finance.

Yet, when I looked at how governments the world over are starting to address the future twin horrors of high graduate unemployment and talent shortages, I found the greatest action so far has been to add more technical skills to curriculums. Computer coding in particular is held up as a panacea for many youth-related issues. Coding is the new language of industry and developed nations are rushing to help children gain fluency in it. There certainly is a need for these skills as much as there is for maths and science, but will this approach truly solve the skills gap in developed economies?

Schools are already well placed to embrace a coding curriculum as it follows a familiar pedagogy: teach, revise and test. It is quantifiable and easy to assess. As ICT classes around the globe get more slots in the timetable, I'm going to play devil's advocate and ask if adding another technical skill to a graduate-saturated world is going to sufficiently narrow the skills gap and provide worthwhile employment in 10 to 20 years' time. Is this the best we can do?

If we apply a little systems thinking to this, it's not too hard to envisage a future, say a decade from now, where there are a great deal more young adults who can code competently. Of course, this allows them to find employment across a wide range of industries as well as the opportunity of being more entrepreneurial with this skill. We'd all love our kids to be the next Zuckerberg or Jobs or the

---

13 At the 2015 World Economic Forum held at Davos, the skills gap was a hot topic discussed at length by representatives of both poor and rich nations.

face of Angry Birds or Minecraft, so bring on coding, right?

An abundance of anything drives down the value. At this trajectory, programmers will become our new assembly line labourers. It's likely that the corporate demand for programmers will be met by 2030 and leave us with a new challenge – finding the skills needed to turn these bits and bytes into ideas and businesses that are sustainable. Let's have a look at the skills fuelling the tech start-ups of today to get an idea of what's working at the moment.

Endeavour Insight[14] is part of a global non-profit that supports high-impact entrepreneurship. Their research confirms what many of us who've been around the city block a few times already suspect – that the average founder of a New York City tech start-up is not a fresh-faced graduate working out of their garage. (New York City is home to the second largest and fastest growing tech hub.) More interestingly, only 35% of these entrepreneurs have technical training in a STEM subject despite STEM education being the very centre of US entrepreneurship policy. You read that correctly: only 35% are technically trained. What on earth are they studying that could be more important or useful in launching a meaningful career at the helm of one's own tech company?

History, philosophy, marketing, business, finance and mostly, economics. Weird, huh? This would have been a good myth for the MythBusters to tackle. They would have found that college dropout CEOs are the exception, not the rule, and that mid-career specialist founders with an average age of 31 who are not technically trained, are the norm. Of course, these founders employ programmers to realise their vision and bring their products to market and in a few years' time, thanks to policy, their

14 Goodwin, M. (2015, January 9). *The myth of the tech whiz who quits college to start a company.* Harvard Business Review. Retrieved from www.endeavor.org/blog/endeavor-insight-and-the-partnership-for-new-york-city-releases-the-power-of-entrepreneur-networks-study-of-nearly-700-industry-trailblazers/

cost of labour may well go down.

An Asia-focused UNESCO report reminds us that "technical skills are the bedrock of industrialisation and so very important in developing economies, but as these economies move up the labour chain and into fully fledged service environments, high-level thinking and behavioural skills largely drive economic growth and job creation."[15]

High-level thinking and behavioural skills! Finally, something tangible that we can really work with. I know what high-level thinking and behavioural skills are, but I want to make sure that I don't fall into the same trap as many education providers do and make these skills something fluffy and abstract and therefore hard to teach. As much as I love the philosophical underpinnings of critical thinking, I don't think companies have this in mind when they look for good thinkers and problem solvers. And I'm pretty sure entrepreneurs aren't up till the wee hours studying the nuances of Nietzsche or the sensibilities of Socrates.

If companies claim that they are ignored by governments and misunderstood by education providers, then let's go straight to where corporates are currently feeling the most pain and the skills that they think they need to heal it and move forward profitably over the next 10 to 15 years. We'll also unpack what high-level thinking and behavioural skills mean to them and what all of this means to you and your children.

---

15 Asia and Pacific Regional Bureau for Education, UNESCO. (2013). *Graduate employability in Asia.*

2.2

CORPORATE FUTURE PROOFING

> ... the idea of the future being different from
> the present is so repugnant to our conventional
> modes of thought and behaviour that most of us
> offer a great resistance to acting on it in practice.
>
> ~ **John Maynard Keynes, 1937**

Imagine a world 15 years from now. That's kind of tricky, isn't it? What makes this even trickier is that to do it as accurately as possible you will need to imagine that you are a political atheist, completely non-dogmatic with no premeditated social views, subscriptions to conventional wisdoms or religious or nationalistic tendencies. In other words, you are completely, absolutely, undoubtedly neutral in all beliefs and mental frames. I know, I know, that's a really tall order and probably impossible to fulfil.

We don't have to imagine that many of us are preparing our dimpled darlings for jobs that don't yet exist in this future world.

Little Adam may grow up to be a dentist like his dad – but in 15 years' time even dentistry will look very different, requiring new skills to harness new laser technologies and cosmetic and other services that haven't yet come to be. We currently assume the most successful dentists of the future will be those with the skills to market and sell lifestyle dentistry products to patients with healthier teeth than ever before.

In information technology, rumours[1] are already circulating that the pixels trapped behind our touchscreens will soon be able to join and interact with us on our side of the world. Inexpensive, interactive 3D platforms without 3D glasses are expected to be the next electronic interface in a future where touchscreens are old school. What comes after that? What will those pixels be doing for us in 15 years' time? What opportunities will they create for future employment? What skills will be needed to exploit them? By their very nature we cannot yet fully conceive of these unknowable jobs of the future, just as our parents could not have imagined us working as a bitcoin trader at a hedge fund on Wall Street.

Corporate management teams are in the unenviable position of having to predict future trends in order to develop corporate and human resource strategies to tackle presumed challenges and maximise currently invisible opportunities. It's no surprise then that a top priority for them is getting a reasonable grasp on what lies beyond the immediately visible horizon. Well-established trends such as ageing populations, the rise of single households, effects of climate change and immersive realities are already, or should be, factors that find their way onto their planning agendas, but these are not the only issues keeping CEOs awake at night.

---

1   Wilson, M. (2014, July 1). *Google is about to take over your whole life, and you won't even notice.* Fast Company. Retrieved from www.fastcodesign.com/3032463/what-is-google

Measuring the pulse of these corporate future proofing concerns around the globe is exactly what the IBM Global C-suite Study does. Every year IBM's researchers conduct interviews with over 4,000 corporate leaders across 70 countries and publish their conclusions at IBM.com. In 2013, every CEO surveyed considered technology the single most important external force shaping their organisations. Don't think for a minute that they were simply referring to leveraging the Internet or building new smartphone apps. No, each one of them, no matter what industry they inhabited, believed that a new digital frontier was emerging that would change how they did business going forward, creating new opportunities and challenges that would need new skills to solve. These new technologies will have greater impact on traditional businesses than Amazon has had on high street stores, Wikipedia has had on access to knowledge or social media has had on critical thinking. This was again echoed in 2014, when *market and technology factors* were singled out as the two most powerful external forces affecting organisations today. By 2015, *disruptive innovation at scale and speed* was seen as the most necessary corporate survival mechanism, relying on training employees with the skill sets to succeed. That's pretty high-level stuff, so let's break it down a little as we peer into the crystal ball of the boardroom.

The digital frontier sits at the intersection between the electronic and physical realms of reality. Digital smart pills, self-healing cars, intelligent clothing and 3D printing of living tissue blur the distinction between virtual and reality into inconsequence. CEOs have little choice but to drive this new source of commercial growth as starry-eyed shareholders wait for their payoffs. Sounds grand, doesn't it? But the technology that CEOs are pontificating about, and basing future revenue streams on, is still in its commercial infancy.

In fact, IBM found that two-thirds of enterprises surveyed still had a weak digital-physical strategy, or none at all. It seems business leaders don't yet know how to strike the right note between the social, digital and physical worlds. Many can't or won't even begin to address this issue until they get their heads around one of the biggest corporate challenges of our century – the monster in the bedroom cupboard, the elephant in the boardroom: data.

CEOs are drowning in the stuff and feel even less equipped to cope with big data than they did three years ago.[2] With our ever more complex and refined digital alter egos that interact, transact and publish ourselves online, the amount of data that is currently generated is staggering. As a species we manufacture as much information every two days as we did from the dawn of civilisation to 2003.[3] David Shenk[4] summed it up perfectly when he wrote, "Information, once rare and cherished like caviar, is now plentiful and taken for granted like potatoes." Any chef can make mashed potatoes but to turn the same potatoes into a dish that distinguishes her restaurant from its competitors and attracts the right numbers of the right customer at the right price requires a real edge in thinking, design and marketing skills and in this case, a flair for flavour.

Only one in five multinational organisations currently has the

2   IBM.com. (2013) *How C-suite executives see the landscape changing.* Retrieved from www-935.ibm.com/services/us/en/c-suite/csuitestudy2013/infographic-01.html

3   Siegler, M.G. (2010, August 4). *Every 2 days we ceate as much information as we did up to 2003.* TechCrunch. Retrieved from www.techcrunch.com/2010/08/04/schmidt-data/

4   Shenk, D. (1997). *Data Smog.* New York, NY: Harper Collins.

capacity to fully utilise their big data.[5] This statistic may deteriorate before it gets better as the volume and variety of our bits and bytes increases with ferocious velocity, faster than our capacity to understand and exploit it. This is information overload on a massive and continuous scale and it really matters to companies and their long-term growth strategies. Not only are leaders expected to make sense of more data but also to understand and engage with more demanding customers. Consumers of goods and services can now injure an otherwise healthy business through bad press on a blog or Facebook, Twitter, Google+, Instagram, YouTube or whatever new information-sharing site is served up before this paragraph reaches you. Chief marketing officers are expected to use and exploit social media tools and technologies their children usually understand better than they do[6] – the same children who are growing up with their heads in digital data clouds.

I don't need to tell you that understanding social media and how it's used to reach consumers is one area where our children already have an inbuilt advantage over older generations. But it's not a real edge at all because their peers are immersed in the same technology. The real edge lies in the ability to make sense of the oceans of data generated by social media and continuously massing on servers around the world. Adults in developed economies are already drowning in information. How do *we* deal with it? Do we have a strategy for beating back its relentless intrusion into our lives, do we know what information to use as inputs in our decision making and what to leave on the sidelines? Are we able to turn potatoes into profit using high-level thinking and behavioural skills? Are we able to teach these skills to our children?

5   Chartered Management Institute and IBM C-suite Study 2013. Retrieved from www-935.ibm.com/services/us/en/c-suite/csuitestudy2013/infographic-01.html
6   IBM.com

A flip around online job sites tells us exactly what high-level thinking and behavioural skills mean to some of the world's most successful and best companies to work for.

In 2014, accounting firm Ernst and Young were looking to fill approximately 16,500 positions. Apart from technical skills and fit with company ethos, what were they after? Their recruiters were honing in on individuals with a passion for problem solving and the ability to tackle complex issues and generate insights. A global mindset is also essential to work across borders in their connected organisation.[7]

Intel is looking for innovative talent; recruits to help spark new thinking that will lead to new ideas.[8] KPMG wants to see candidates who are able to use social media to their advantage. They recommend that candidates post comments on Twitter that show their expertise, have a professional-looking LinkedIn profile with appropriate recommendations, and participate in chat forums of professional interest.[9] Fashion house Nordstrom is looking for curious and innovative candidates.[10]

Adobe takes skill requirements one step further with the requirement that candidates are able to demonstrate strong emotional intelligence alongside the capacity to drive innovation.[11] Genentech adds that the ability to demonstrate smart risk taking, even if it failed, is a valuable asset to them.[12]

7   CNN interview with Larry Nash, executive recruiting leader at Ernst & Young. Retrieved from money.cnn.com/gallery/news/companies/2014/01/16/best-companies-hiring.fortune/

8   CNN interview with Christy Dickenson, regional manager for global talent acquisition at Intel. Retrieved from money.cnn.com/gallery/news/companies/2014/01/16/best-companies-hiring.fortune/3.html

9   Interview with KPMG recruiting manager Christina Tran, by Christopher Tkaczyk. (2014, January 16). Retrieved from Fortune.com.

10   Retrieved from money.cnn.com/gallery/news/companies/2014/01/16/best-companies-hiring.fortune/9.html

11   Interview with Jeff Vijungco, Adobe's vice president of global talent. Retrieved from money.cnn.com/gallery/news/companies/2014/01/16/best-companies-hiring.fortune/9.html

12   Interview with Amanda Valentino, director of corporate staffing at Genentech. Retrieved from money.cnn.com/gallery/news/companies/2014/01/16/best-companies-hiring.fortune/9.html

I was a guest at a recent tech conference at Microsoft's UK headquarters in the Thames Valley (the Silicon Valley of Europe) along with several heads of leading technology companies. The topic that dominated the morning discussion was the state of the skills gap in technology. It was astounding to see the very real effect that this was having on these companies in terms of their bottom line. Very few of them knew what to do about it other than apprenticeships. To cheer us up a bit, we were introduced to software that allowed us all to reply to questions from the speakers and panellists on our smartphones. We could then see on the projector screens what everyone else had responded. I took a screen shot of the replies to the question, "What skills are lacking from job applicants?" and here were the responses[13] given:

- Motivation, ambition, personality
- Problem solving, creative thinking
- Critical Thinking
- HTML5, CSS and SQL
- Creativity
- Collaboration
- Ability to achieve results using technology
- Grit and determination
- Desire to contribute more than anything else
- Active listening
- Passion and enthusiasm
- Communication skills
- Ability to articulate verbally
- Languages

---

13 2016 Thames Valley Tech Conference organised by the Thames Valley Chamber of Commerce.

- Collaborative communication
- Entrepreneurial skills
- Creative thinking
- Critical thinking and analysis

Look at that! Only one respondent asked for programing languages whilst the majority are crying out for soft skills, most notably communication skills.

Even traditional hard skill industries are feeling the need for something a bit softer. Auditing giants KMPG and PricewaterhouseCoopers admitted to *The Sunday Age* that soft skills were now valued more highly than technical ability.[14] According to KPMG, the Internet is the new font of technical knowledge, freeing up our brains to do more interesting things than remember vast quantities of data. "How you collaborate, solve problems creatively and authentically lead people will matter more," says Susan Ferrier, KPMG's national managing partner – people, performance and culture.

And when it comes to recruitment processes, Google is leading the way in showing the world how to hire the best of the best in a post-grades world.

---

14 Elder, J. (2015, March 15). The rise of soft skills: why top marks no longer get the best jobs. *The Sunday Age.*

2.3

THE CV IS DEAD, LONG LIVE AI

Did you know that it's easier to get into Harvard than Google? Your or your child's odds of getting to work at one of the world's most desirable employers with the all-you-can-eat-for-free organic deli at the Googleplex and its many miniplexes around the world, are 1 in 130. The odds of getting into one of the most hallowed academic institutions known to our generation, Harvard, are a mere 1 in 14. Google gets over 1 million job applicants a year and employs 0.4% to 0.5% of them. Their internship is 2,600% oversubscribed.[1] It must be the free lunches.

In a company that produces the purest, most valuable data that money can buy, it's no surprise that their recruitment processes have benefitted from their lead in analytics. Laszlo Bock, their former Senior Vice President of People Operations and principal architect of their recruiting process made headlines when he revealed what most Googlers already know: that academic success at college or one's GPA (grade point average) is the least important metric in their interview process. In fact, he went on to say that it is discounted in the final selection stage.[2]

---

1 An average of 40,000 applicants apply for the 1,500 positions. The number is rising too.
2 Laszlo Bock gave insights into their hiring process at an interview on March 28, 2013 at *The Economist's Ideas Economy: Innovation Forum* in Berkeley, California

He didn't say so simply to be cool and contrarian. He doesn't need to because their 16 years' worth of data on recruitment have revealed that there is no link between formal academic success or technical ability and potential to add real value to a company that transacts in new technology. What they hire for is the ability to learn, mental agility and someone who is not held hostage by years of deep specialisation in a particular area.

Google is all grown up now and their recruitment process is unashamedly geared towards identifying candidates who will create the future – without being evil – of course. So when Laszlo Bock says they are looking for curiosity, intellectual humility and resilience, he isn't saying so because it sounds all Googly but because he knows this is what has brought them to where they are and will take them forward. Plus, they have found a way of testing for this through their behaviour-based interview process.

Bock highlights resilience several times. Someone who has known academic success most of their life has probably never gotten down and dirty with failure and so might well be crushed by it. Internally, Google fails a lot, that's the nature of exploring unchartered territory. Without resilience, no new app or technology would be brought to life.

In a bout of intellectual humility, Bock admitted that their previous, infamous, interviewing idiosyncrasies that included asking bizarre questions like how many cows there were in Canada, were one of these failures. "A complete waste of time. They don't predict anything and serve primarily to make the interviewer feel smart," he admits. Well, that's good news, especially if your child wants to work at Google. But what if he wanted to work somewhere else? Is this discounting of GPAs and 15 years of expensive education just a Google thing? Nope, it seems to be a growing trend. A trend that is sucking the life out of an old faithful of corporate recruiting: the formal curriculum vitae. A relic of the pre-electronic age, it seems to be going the way of big hair and platform shoes as it retreats into the ever lengthening shadows of the digital world.

In February 2015, French cosmetics giant L'Oreal was faced with 33,000 applications for the 70 places available in their Chinese graduate recruitment scheme. At the thought of combing through 33,000 CVs, their recruiters decided that it was time to do things differently. "Don't send us your CV," they announced, "we won't read it." Instead, they directed candidates to three online questions that they should answer instead. Here's one of those questions, compliments of the BBC and L'Oreal: "If you had one month and a 25,000RMB budget ($4,000; £2,570) to tackle any project your little heart desired, what would you do?"[3]

What? How dare they? There was no call for the name of the school applicants graduated from, their chemistry scores, language proficiency or greatest hopes and biggest failures. The answers to those three questions in 75 words or less were analysed by artificial intelligence. Suitable candidates were then ranked in terms of the qualities most desired by L'Oreal. Only 500 of the initial applicants were invited for Skype interviews thereafter. L'Oreal's recruitment director confessed that CVs don't give insight into what they are really after in students – raw talent.

Unfortunately, all these skills we've been chatting about aren't yet staples in classrooms. But don't worry, I'm not going to suggest

3   Sudworth, J. (2015, February 25). Can technology identify China's top graduates? *BBC News China*.

that you crack open the Lego and task your 3-year-old with finding patterns in random heaps of plastic on the rug or see a therapist to get a handle on his temper tantrums. I am going to help you help your children think in alternative ways about information. Especially in areas where you don't know the answer or there is no answer to know. Guiding them into mentally uncomfortable situations armed with a cognitive Swiss army knife is as valuable as the best education your money can buy to prepare them for this brave new world.

TIPS AND TAKEAWAYS FROM CHAPTER 2

Chapter 2 was a cloudburst of information with lots for you to think about. If you ask me what we really need to remember about our children's future, I'd say it's the skills they will need to be economically active as young adults. This could be in traditional corporate roles, as entrepreneurs or something in between.

We spoke at length about *high-level thinking* and *behavioural skills*. If these words are starting to sound like the soulless jargon tossed around boardrooms, then here's a summary of what the corporate world actually means when they ask for these skills and why.

1. Systems thinking

As big data continues to swell, the current need for both employees and entrepreneurs that can simplify complexity will swell too. A knack for interpreting data and drawing conclusions to inform innovation is already a sought-after skill. A good grasp of systems thinking and the ability to model first and second order consequences from innovation become the natural next step in skills requirements.

2. Risk and failure

When working with unchartered ideas, risk and failure are part of the package. It helps if recruits understand that these are prerequisites to pioneering disruptive change and indispensable for start-ups. The ability to take measured risk is already on the hit list of forward-looking recruiters like those at Google – a company with a high product failure rate that they are particularly proud of. "Have you failed before?" and "How did you deal with it?" are popular interview questions. They want to know about that one time, back in 2010, when you failed spectacularly, how you coped with the personal blow and what you did to get back on track. Not when you lost the spelling bee in the 7th grade or missed out on being class rep.

3. Global exposure

Most organisations are either global or want to be global. Young adults who have been exposed to a global community have a head start. Not just having a couple of Korean friends at college (or American friends if you're Korean) but actually having worked with or explored countries with diverse cultures. And I don't mean being a tourist in Paris for Easter weekend, but spending a summer somewhere exotic, interning on the other side of the world, taking a gap year abroad or even doing immersive cultural (think six months on a *kibbutz* in Israel) or language studies. None of this is essential, of course, but very valuable in the beady eyes of a multinational recruiter. "More and more employers are wanting graduates to have a 'global mindset', which means understanding different cultures and how industries work across borders," says Stephen Isherwood, chief executive of the Association of Graduate Recruiters.

4. Innovation and problem solving

Previously, most of us were rewarded for being productive. Being creative was the role of the R&D or marketing department. Today, figuring out how to get the job done faster and more cost effectively, solving customer complaints in smarter ways and always being on the lookout for the next best idea are sought-after skills in every area.

The corporate world is acutely aware that creativity is required to drive economic growth across developed countries. Yet, in Adobe's large and sombre State of Create Study,[4] there is universal concern across developed nations that school is stifling this most important skill. We'll talk much more about this later on as well as how to foster a creative mindset.

5. Behavioural smarts

Technical skills are a given but behavioural skills such as emotional and social intelligence are increasingly required even for entry-level positions where engagement with colleagues and clients requires a cool head or the ability to influence, not just sell. If your

---

4   Adobe State of Create Study. (2012). Retrieved from Adobe.com

child has an eye on becoming the "boss" of anything, even his own lemonade stand, then emotional smarts must feature on his curriculum. I'll show you how a little later.

Given that employability today and tomorrow is as much about maths scores as it is about adaptability, resilience and social, emotional and raw intelligence, what are our schools doing about fostering these talents? Why is there still not a grade for emotional intelligence and innovation that actually contributes to a child's final grade on his annual report card? Are they addressing the need for both hard and soft skills? What can we reasonably expect from the hardworking dedicated folk who are educating the day after tomorrow's global leaders, entrepreneurs, soldiers and nurses?

Note to the school-wise: if you already know how your child's school system influences his ability to think critically or you don't care how school systems around the world differ, then please jump right over Chapter 3 and head on to the practical stuff from Chapter 4 onwards. This is a how-to guide after all.

3.1

SCHOOLS IN THE LAND OF PISA

With minds focused on the future and eyes trained on exams, anything unrelated to the syllabus is considered an irrelevant distraction. The word "why" fills my students with dread. Being asked their own views gives them panic attacks. It cannot be said enough that we should teach students to think, not just to learn the syllabus but all they want is to follow the rulebook and pass exams.

> ~ **The Secret Teacher,**
> **who teaches a humanities subject in an**
> **"outstanding" sixth-form college**
> **in an affluent area of the UK,**
> **writing in *The Guardian*, 7 February 2015**

Throughout my eight years in Singapore, I worked with executives in various companies across different industries on the subject of critical thinking, behavioural finance and decision making in leadership. In 2009, I began working with the Monetary Authority of Singapore – Singapore's central bank – where I created and taught an MBA-style programme on critical thinking and decision making for their staff. For part of that time, I taught critical thinking at an international business school with students hailing from 21 different countries across the East and West, North and South. They had different accents, experiences and ways of thinking and being from different national values, beliefs and school systems.

It has long been thought that different people learn in different ways. Some students learn better from visuals, others from stories while some prefer facts and data. What I didn't expect to find was that achievement in my subject seemed to be influenced as much by nationality as individual strengths and weaknesses. What was even more interesting was that students' achievement in my critical-thinking classes seemed uncorrelated with their grades in other subjects, especially technical subjects. This was by no means a rigorous study but it was backed up by my experience in the corporate sector as well.

After a decade in Asia I had discovered a consistency in how students and course participants from different countries used their thinking tools and approached problems. For example, Japanese students would often gather so much data that they ran out of time to make conclusions. My Indian students usually had their hands up first and were very comfortable with offering answers even if they didn't have enough data to fully substantiate them – to many of them, a hunch was data too. To be clear this wasn't a reflection of intelligence or work ethic – smart, hardworking individuals and the opposite were found across all nationalities. This was about people conforming to nationalistic frames in their thinking about subjects that didn't touch on tradition, religion or nationalism. Of course there were exceptions, but they were just that.

I grew increasingly curious about how this systemic phenomenon occurred and why. My curiosity led me to look a little closer at the various school systems that produced such consistent thinking across national cohorts. Even between Asian countries the spectrum of thinking styles was substantially diverse yet specific enough to each nationality to be noticed. It puzzled me – a lot. Were there nationalities that were better critical and lateral thinkers than others? It certainly seemed so from my own sampling over a reasonable time frame. Who were they? I'll give you a hint, they hailed from countries where innovation is high and maths and science scores in the PISA tests aren't.

PISA? Not that of the Leaning Tower fame but the Program for International Student Assessment conducted by the Paris-based Organisation for Economic Cooperation and Development who you may know as the OECD. Every three years they assess the maths, science and reading ability of more than half a million 15- and 16- year-old students in 65 countries and cities, representing 80% of the world economy. Shanghai, China has been at the very top of the tables since 2009 when it began participating. Results published in December 2013 were that of the 2012 testing series focusing on maths with Singapore coming in 2nd and Hong Kong 3rd for maths behind Shanghai (China) in pole position. All top performers were of Chinese, also known as Confucian, heritage. Confucian heritage countries are those heavily influenced by traditional Chinese culture and include China, Korea, Singapore,

Hong Kong and Taiwan. The US came in at 36th and the UK at 26th (near the OECD average) out of 65 in maths.

So, I had been working in an education superpower, a country hailed as having produced one of the top three education systems in the world as far as maths, science and reading go. Yet in my experience, I found that basic lateral and critical thinking challenged my Confucian heritage, and especially Singaporean, students to the brink of giving up.

Surely one of the best education systems in the world would be producing innovative and agile thinkers en masse?

Smart they were, exceptionally smart. Technically they ran cognitive rings around the Australian, British, American and even mainland Chinese students in my lectures. They scoffed at my feeble maths challenges. But when it came to turning problems upside down, reframing data, innovating or purposefully engaging metacognition, they grew quiet, waiting for me to offer more framework or more instruction on what tools or methodologies they were meant to use. They were bursting with technical data and models yet I was looking for something else entirely.

Here's an example of an introductory problem that many of my students struggled with. It is also the first exercise we do in the very first class before we even get to know each other.

Exercise

Time allowed: 15 minutes

You and three colleagues run a small IT start-up in Singapore, with huge potential to grow. You have just pitched prototype technology to a new, and potentially, very large client – RIM (Research in

Motion). RIM is looking for an Asian partner to produce innovative parts for a new smartphone. The presentation goes well and the client seems very eager to move on to price negotiations as their time in Singapore is limited. After your presentation they request a 30-minute break. Thereafter they would like to continue and discuss pricing, exclusivity, deliverables and time frames. Your team is not prepared for this as the product is not in mass production yet. You would need at least a month to investigate and gather this information after funding is secured.

The less experienced members of your team start to panic. You feel that winning this account is crucial to the success of your start-up.

Task: In 10 minutes, decide what you will do with the 30 minutes allotted to you. Use any tools and information accessible to you.

What would you do? You may well have found yourself in a similar situation with colleagues or clients. It seems unreasonable, but it happens. Both MBA students and more seasoned corporate leaders usually acted on this information in similar ways.

Because time was short, the dominant voice in the group would usually tell everyone else what had to be done. Delivery time frames had to be ascertained by calling part suppliers and manufacturers. Pricing had to be finalised by doing some nifty calculations on the fly. Many would call their office to get figures that were waiting for them there. You get the picture. Most of them got busy and did the very best that they could to meet the client's demands. Because most of them assumed that this is what I, the lecturer, was looking for.

Only very few participants would sit back and ask themselves why would such a large handset manufacturer put them (a really small start-up) under such pressure to determine deliverables and prices for an unproven product? Should the scenario itself be questioned? A few of these doubtful individuals even jumped onto Google to have a look at the state of RIM's financials. RIM was hardly in a good financial position; it hadn't been for years and really couldn't afford to back speculative technology. Given this, exclusivity clauses should have been out of the question. Very few students concluded that they didn't want the business and would rather walk away than cut a speedy deal with an unsound partner.

The majority of students never actually questioned the deal or the client. They wanted to make the deal happen and tried to show me that they were capable of making it work. They assumed this is what was expected of them. If you look at the question carefully, you will see that *they* were the ones who thought the deal was important, not me. I wanted to see them question their own motivation and mental frames and that of the RIM executives. Why were they being pushed into such a small corner by such a large manufacturer? Would their start-up even benefit from such a deal? The students that jumped right in to serve the client and wrap up the deal displayed goal-orientated behaviour and I saw it again and again in my Confucian heritage students. Yet, a few others were able to sit back and ponder the bigger picture. These students already showed a spark of the critical in their thinking and proved to be the process-orientated ones in my programmes.

I know, I tossed them into the deep end in the first hour of the course. Students either loved or hated me thereafter. Some swam but most of them sank like stones. At school, these students had been taught to calculate a solution from within the constraints presented and not to question the constraints. My job was a tough one, to reprogramme much of the mental conditioning that had been done at schools or in their workplace. They had developed an outcome- or goal-orientation to ensure that they achieve assessable results to definable problems. For almost all of them, their academic success was defined by their test scores. School had taught them what to think to beat the test. How else would you get the best maths score in a class of the world's brightest? But critical thinking is the ability to think about one's thinking: how to think, not what to think.

Confucian heritage societies have been outcome-orientated since the 10th century. By passing imperial China's imperial examinations anyone, from any walk of life or trade, could become a government official. Position and ranking would be based on test scores alone. Later, through the Song Dynasty, achievement in formal tests became the only way to advance in one's career. This system of being able to clearly define and measure someone's aptitude based on explicit metrics seems to have stuck. In a country of 1.3 billion people with cities like Shanghai at 23 million strong, heaving under 9,700 inhabitants per square mile, perhaps this is not surprising at all.

Globally, PISA ranking are a great big deal – attractive enough to encourage power players from "poorer performing" school systems around the world to visit the top scorers. Armed with iPads and notepads, under the influence of jet lag, men and women from the West visit in the hope of bottling the magic formula that makes these Asian children the smartest in the world[1] and carrying it back to their institutions in the US and Europe. Two months after PISA results were released in December 2013, representatives from the UK's Department of Education jetted off to Shanghai on a fact-finding mission with plans to adjust the UK's education policy based on their findings.

> [UK Education Secretary] Mrs Nicky Morgan's target is for England's schools to catch up with international competitors and to enter the top five of the PISA tests in English and maths by 2020.
>
> ~ **BBC News, 2 February 2015**

The 2012 PISA test was presented by commentators as a test of critical thinking.[2] As proud as Asia is of their results (and so they should be) I do look around me and wonder where all these thousands of critical thinking children are when they become adults? In Singapore, it is a cliché that students cannot think outside the box because they spend so much time (almost all of their school career) being taught to navigate the box itself. I wanted to understand this conundrum and unravel the mystery of the missing critical thinkers. The best place to start was the PISA test itself.

Am I smarter than a 15-year-old? This is what I was wondering as I sat to answer the 26 maths questions released by PISA from their test.[3] To be honest, I was merely hoping to qualify as being *as smart* as a 15-year-old. It's been a while since I had to do times tables, or any calculation for that matter, in my head. Taking the

---

1   Ripley, A. (2013). *The Smartest Kids in the World and How They Got That Way*. New York, NY: Simon & Schuster

2   Alliance for Excellent Education. (2013, November 27). PISA 101 Interview with Robert Rothman by Cyndi Waite.

3   The PISA test material is copyrighted and cannot be reproduced here. However, for a little catch up with high school maths and let's not forget old Pythagoras, it's worth a trip to www.oecd.org/pisa/pisaproducts/pisa2012-2006-rel-items-maths-ENG.pdf

test alone, with no clock ticking already put me at an advantage, but I still felt a little nervous as I thumbed through the question sheet. "My students will never know my result," I reminded myself and cracked a wicked grin as I popped on my critical-thinking hat and turned the first page.

But it soon became clear that I didn't need my special hat at all. Question 1 asked me the best way of calculating the floor area of a pretty standard apartment. Not the actual floor area, just how to do it. The next tested my understanding of formulas involving fractions (what happens to the answer if one number in the numerator changes). It certainly helped that my son's homework that week had been fractions. I nailed that one without a blink (the PISA equation, not my son's homework, of course). I cruised along through questions about sailing ships using wind power to cut costs and the progress of Ferris wheel passengers.

Just as I was thinking, "Gosh, I'm good", I hit a snag at question 8 – determining the length of one side of a triangle based on the length of the other two sides. Uh? Time for a coffee break and a sneaky peak at Wikipedia to search for the name of the chap that came up with the formula to calculate the length of the longest side of a triangle. You know, the side opposite the right angle? The *hypotenuse*. Hello, Pythagoras. This was the only theorem that the 26 questions called for. The rest of the sample questions were much the same and followed a pretty predictable approach:

1. Decide on the calculation you need to perform
2. Choose the correct variables from the information given
3. Calculate and record

I couldn't help but wonder where the critical thinking component was. Or was my definition of critical thinking a little too narrow?

Make no mistake, it was a refreshing challenge, like a brisk morning walk through the snow, barefoot. But at no point did I feel the need to get out the shovel and uncover some facts for myself or examine the problem from multiple angles. Everything I needed was handed to me. Here are examples of the questions that the OECD singled out to illustrate the various levels of difficulty they tested at. To respect their copyright, I have paraphrased them using alternative objects and variables but the methods and level of difficulty remain the same. Here is an example of the Level 5 (second hardest level) question. See if you can work it out?

Example Test Question (Level 5)

Mount Fuji is the highest mountain in Japan. There are several trails that lead up to the summit. Gotemba trail is 9km to the summit. Hikers are required to return to the start of the trail before sunset at 7 p.m. Thea is about to hike this trail and estimates that she can walk up at 2km per hour and down at twice that speed inclusive of breaks. What is the latest time she must start walking the 18km-trail so that she is back at base before sunset?

Not too hard, is it? Did you need abstract reasoning or critical-thinking skills? Nope, you didn't.

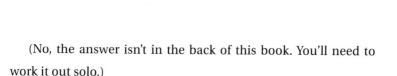

(No, the answer isn't in the back of this book. You'll need to work it out solo.)

At the heart of critical thinking lies reasoning, judgement and metacognition, which is thinking about one's thinking process. Critical thinking involves the following abilities:

1. Understanding the context and frames within which a problem occurs

2. Spotting assumptions and other unstated influences or relationships

3. Gathering evidence and evaluating it in light of points 1 and 2 above

4. Using reflective thinking (metacognition) to consider the influence of one's own mental frames and biases

5. Using appropriate tools and techniques to generate solutions

6. Evaluating solutions with reference to the above

7. Testing solutions

I know that this is a great deal for any 15-year-old to master. But these skills weren't required to complete this Level 5 question. What was needed was the ability to abstract real-world data and create a mathematical problem to solve using basic maths – all essential life skills. Did you need to understand context and frames? How about assumptions? Gathering evidence? Nope. OK, maybe a Level 5 question is not where the critical thinking came in. Let's try a Level 6 example question, the highest level. Got your pen, paper and critical-thinking hat ready?

Example Test Question (Level 6)

Araj has a new bicycle. It took Araj 9 minutes to pedal to the mall which is 4km away. He returned home via a shortcut of only 3km which took him 6 minutes. What was his average speed for the trip to the mall and back?

You tell me, is this a critical-thinking question? Again, the ability to extract and link information tied to real-world problems is essential. Students would have had to develop a strategy for approaching it logically, but after that, it's basic maths again. After going through all their representative questions, the light bulb flickered and I started understanding why teens from Confucian heritage societies were doing so well.

The highest percentage of students who attained Level 6 were from Shanghai (31%) followed by 19% of Singaporean students. The OECD average was 3% as was the UK score whilst only 2% of US students tested attained Level 6. The top seven countries were all Asian countries. As evidenced by the level of attainment, this maths paper is a real challenge for any 15-year-old. However, it is not a test of critical thinking but an application of previously learnt methods to problems one would encounter in the "real-world".

Singapore and China are both Confucian heritage societies with similar school systems. From primary school onwards, children are moved and placed according to test results only. Remember the imperial examination system? This makes sense in a system that regularly loads one teacher with 40 pupils. Students are wise to focus on attaining the best test results from a very early age.[4] Historically, Confucianism has fostered personal effort and discipline as the building blocks of success, not innate ability, with the belief that any child can be at the top of their class – if they work harder than their classmates. The opposite is also true: if a child is not at the top of their class, they aren't working hard enough. Parental involvement is high at home but not at school. In Singapore, parents regularly take maths classes so that they can give their kids an edge in exams. In Shanghai, at the time of writing this, many teachers are incentivised with bonuses based on their students' test scores alone.

It's no surprise then that these students can spend seven days a week on study, revision and homework, learning test techniques and practising papers. This phenomenon is further fuelled by the general acceptance that tutoring is an integral part of education. These children are not being trained to be future visionaries, entrepreneurs or researchers but rather exceptionally hard workers who can navigate and work the testing system better than most.

Given incentivisation structures, high teacher/student ratios and fierce academic competition, there remains much political and parental pressure on schools and teachers to provide testing that can be reliably and uncontroversially graded. This advocates closed or multiple-choice questions. Neither of which encourage creative or critical thinking.[5]

4   Emma Vanbergen, Shanghai-based study abroad director for BE Education, a company that places Chinese pupils in British education. (2011, December 4). *The Telegraph.*
5   Carless, D. (2011). *From Testing to Productive Student Learning: Implementing Formative Assessment in Confucian Heritage Settings.* London: Routledge

But what happens after their rigorous schooling? It seems that many go off to study abroad. In fact, China is the world's largest exporter of students. The number of Asian students studying at American tertiary institutions is currently up by more than 20% year on year.[6] This growth is expected to taper off as more options open up for them at home with American and European universities taking advantage of an obvious revenue stream by setting up campus on Asian shores.

When is a Goldfish Not Dead?

I was fortunate to interview Judy,[7] a Singapore-based British expatriate and education consultant who is in the uncommon position of having her son schooled first at an international school in Singapore and then at a local state school. This is rather rare as special permission must be obtained for expatriate children to study in local schools. The same goes for Singaporean children who wish to study at international schools. She retells the tale of a child's attempt at answering an English comprehension test at a Singaporean school at Primary 2 level (at the age of 7- to 8-years-old). It went like this:

Excerpt from a paragraph: "... and the cat ate the goldfish"
Question: What happened to the goldfish?
Answer by pupil: The goldfish died.

Surely a most natural conclusion to being eaten by a cat, written in a satisfactorily full sentence. Yet this answer was marked as incorrect by the English teacher. Naturally, the student's mother asked for clarity. The correct answer, she was told, was that the

---

6   Institute of International Educations' Open Doors (2013). Retrieved from www.iie.org/
7   Not her real name.

fish was eaten by the cat. Death was implied when in fact there was no proof of it. Thus, there could only be one correct answer.

With PISA 2012's focus on maths, it's little wonder Asian schools are at the top of the charts. If you plant apple seeds, water, prune and protect them, then you are going to get beautiful apples. But only apples. If education has such a narrow definition of excellence, do we not lose our visionaries, our dreamers? The ones who are going to break the moulds so that something new and better can be developed (and coded by the very smart kids with perfect maths scores)?

China itself has recognised the need to reform their school system. A government document[8] issued in 2001 called for schools to move away from pure knowledge transmission using repetitive and mechanistic rote-learning towards increased student participation in a more relevant, real-world curriculum. They also recognised the need to de-emphasise the screening and selective functions of assessments and instead to emphasise their formative and constructive functions. This is a Herculean task because real change in this system requires defiance of centuries of Confucian heritage programming re-enforced by enviable and clearly measurable results.

Many Chinese complain scathingly that their system kills independent thought and creativity, and they envy the American system for nurturing self-reliance – and for trying to make learning exciting and not just a chore.

~ **Robert Kirkpatrick,**
Shinawatra International University, Thailand

---

8 Ministry of Education of The PRC. (2001). *Framework for the Curriculum Reform of Basic Education – The Trial Version*

If children raised in Confucian heritage countries are leaving school with a high level of technical proficiency and a disciplined goal-orientation, but a lack of critical- and creative-thinking skills, what are children in other major centres such as the US and UK taking with them as they leave mission control at high school?

Additional resources

The Negative Influences of Exam-Oriented Education on Chinese High School Students: Backwash from Classroom to Child by Robert Kirkpatrick and Yuebing Zang, Shinawatra International University, Thailand. Published in Language Testing in Asia, October 2011.

3.2

COMPARING APPLES
AND PEARS

According to PISA, American scholars leave with very little that
will prepare them for life in the unknown: "Students in the United
States have particular strengths in cognitively less-demanding
mathematical skills and abilities, such as extracting single values
from diagrams or handling well-structured formulae. They have
particular weaknesses in items with higher cognitive demands,
such as taking real-world situations, translating them into
mathematical terms, and interpreting mathematical aspects in
real-world problems."[1] The US spends more education dollars
per student than most countries, yet this does not translate into
better performance. The Slovak Republic, which spends around
$53,000 per student, performed at the same level as the United
States, which spends over $115,000 per student.

The full findings for the US paint a pretty gloomy report,
one that would have had a Shanghainese student sat behind
shame curtains for a week. It reports that the United States has
a below-average share of top performers in mathematics. These
are students that can develop and work with models for complex

---

1   PISA US. (2012).

situations and work strategically using broad, well-developed thinking and reasoning skills. Only 2% of students in the United States reach the highest level (Level 6) of performance in mathematics, compared with an OECD average of 3% and 31% of students in Shanghai, China. The proportion of top performers in reading and science in the US are both around the OECD average.

Despite wide-ranging reforms, the United States' results in maths, science and reading haven't changed significantly since 2006. Yet America's ability to drive innovation and contribute to various scientific fields remains robust. The US contributes 6 of the top 10 companies and 24 of the top 50 on the 2014 Forbes[2] list of most innovative companies. China owns none in the top 10 and only 6 of the top 50. Of course, there are many metrics and even more surveys that slice and dice innovation data differently. There are even metrics that measure a country's contribution to science directly such as the rather sensible – though not free of criticism – H-Index, a ranking that reflects not only the quantity of articles published by a country's scientists or scholars but also the number of times they were cited by researchers. Citations are considered a measure of quality and usefulness. China ranks 17th in the H-Index. The top 10 spots are populated by countries whose school children largely muddle around the OECD average in science. Interesting, isn't it?

So, let's compare apples with pears and look at the scientific contributions of a nation's adults with the current PISA rankings of their teenagers. Here are the 2015 H-Index rankings[3] for all subjects with the 2012 overall PISA ranking in brackets next to it.

---

2 Retrieved from www.forbes.com/innovative-companies/list/
3 Rankings taken for all subjects from the SJR (Scimago Journal Rank). Retrieved from www. scimagojr.com/countryrank

H-INDEX RANKING	(PISA RANKING)
1. USA	(36th)
2. UK	(26th)
3. Germany	(16th)
4. France	(26th)
5. Canada	(13th)
6. Japan	(7th)
7. Italy	(32nd)
8. Netherlands	(10th)
9. Switzerland	(9th)
10. Australia	(19th)

Singapore came in at 25th on the H-Index and Hong Kong at 26th with China (not Shanghai alone) creeping up the ranks at 14th.

China, Singapore and Hong Kong are glaringly absent from the top 10 H-Index rankings. The bottom line is that schools get ranked on results that can be measured in any academic year for a specific cohort. It is overwhelmingly logical that students and teachers maximise these results. Are US, UK and German schools superior? I have no metrics to support such a claim. If we can't claim any school system is superior over the long haul, then what can we take away from this data? Firstly, that no school system is perfect. Secondly, it becomes clear that we can't leave it to any school system to raise our children with a complete and competent skill set.

Around the world parents have very little influence over the policies that will shape their children's academic future. Maybe you are a parent in Hong Kong who would like to see more diversity in the curriculum, or a British parent who wants to see Mandarin instead of French in the syllabus or an immigrant American parent who desperately wants his child to learn resilience and the ability to wrestle with real-world problems using critical analysis? If so, you are not alone and you are not powerless over your child's outcomes.

If you and I are stuck with government school systems from China to the US, it may well be up to us to fill in the glaring gaps in what and how our children are being taught. To equip them with skills to navigate an uncertain future and use their mental superpowers to their fullest. Fortunately, teaching them *how* to think while they learn *what* to think is easier than you think.

TIPS AND TAKEAWAYS FROM CHAPTER 3

1. Try not to get overly distraught or elated about your country's PISA ranking. The proof of the PISA pudding is whether an education system can foster the skills needed to innovate and maintain economic growth in the medium to long term. These are skills not currently measured by PISA.

2. If your child's school is not able to teach her high-level thinking and behavioural skills (you know what these are by now) then you'll have to do it yourself, mom or dad, if you want her to be successful in her chosen pursuits.

3. A fish will in fact die if it's eaten by a cat.

PART 2

RAISING THINKERS

4.1

THE PARENT COACH

> If children are taught to make decisions
> from a young age, they will experience the
> consequences of their choices more often and so
> learn to make better decisions as they mature.
>
> **~ Sir John Whitmore**

When my son was 6-years-old, I had a very uncomfortable realisation: I was better at being an executive coach than a parent. The evidence was incontrovertible: my coaching clients looked forward to our sessions, did their homework, never ignored me or called me names. I never, ever had to yell at them to get them to pay attention. We got stuff done together and afterwards some of them wrote lovely notes or LinkedIn recommendations for me and we caught up annually for coffee. But at home it didn't always go so well. I had been dubbed the *mom-enator* (terminator mom – even worse than a tiger mom).

I really couldn't understand why I could help adults change behaviours, achieve their goals and navigate toxic business environments – but I couldn't get my son to take pride in his schoolwork, or even just do his homework, without me having to nag him. Have you ever been in this position with your children? If so, you'll know it's not pretty.

In typical parent mode, I had tried to change my son through encouraging, asking, lecturing, bribing, ordering, yelling and finally withholding pocket money and/or iPad/TV/Xbox time. Yet my success rate and return on time invested with him was pitiful. By any corporate measures of ROI, I would have failed spectacularly as a parent. How could I help him be a better thinker if we couldn't get past the five times table without tension?

At the lowest point in our relationship, I realised that the problem was not him, it was me. I was trying to make him want to be better and make him improve his attitude towards learning. And, far worse than that, I had accused him of upsetting me. I would never even consider using any of these tactics in coaching because I know they don't work and aren't allowed anyway. Besides, no one can make me angry or upset; I have to choose to be angry. Yet all was not lost. I was a coach after all and knew how to use coaching methodology to nudge behavioural changes. I was willing to bet the class kitty[1] that it would work magic on my ability to influence my son and his future.

Executive coaches are trained to help clients identify and overcome obstacles and fears and succeed in their chosen pursuits. Parents are trained in... well, I've never met a parent who's trained in parenting. Imagine that – a professional parent? Not a stay-at-home mum, dad or home executive but someone with a diploma or degree in the most important and dynamic field

---

1   As the class treasurer for two years, I never bet the kitty on anything. Just a figure of speech.

today – parenting. I'm better trained as a coach than a parent so should stick to what I know best. It's no surprise then that when I changed my parenting style to a coaching style, it worked.

If you aren't familiar with the booming executive coaching industry, let's step aside for a minute and look at the numbers underpinning its popularity. I would love to present you with sexy statistics showing the phenomenal success rate of executive coaching, but success in coaching is incredibly subjective. Creating a statistically significant sample of coachees (those receiving coaching) willing to talk about why they were coached and how successful the coaching was would be tricky, to say the least. So here's what we can measure: the 2013 Executive Coaching Survey[2] conducted by the Centre for Leadership Development and Research at Stanford Graduate School of Business tells us that 34% of CEOs and 51% of senior executives receive coaching. Forty-three percent of respondents in a different study[3] confirmed that their organisation employed internal coaches and 60% said coaching was available to their high-potential employees including those still in lower levels of management. Clearly there is a demand for coaching. Given that it is significantly more expensive per hour than soft-skills training, I like to think that this demand exists because it works better than training.

The basic principles that coaches use with their clients can be used by you at home to guide and empower your children from the bouncy castle to the boardroom, and you don't need any special qualification to get started. In your quest to raise your children as thinkers, this is possibly the most important advice I can give you. So listen up.

---

2 In conjunction with Stanford University's Rock Centre for Corporate Governance and The Miles Group.
3 ICF and the Human Capital Institute. (2014). *Building a Coaching Culture.*

Firstly, a couple of things had to change in how I interacted with my son. In executive coaching, the relationship between the coach and the coachee is one of the primary determinants of the success of that coaching engagement. Companies spend a lot of money on executive coaches and so spend a lot of time finding the right coach for each employee. Connection, mutual respect, trust and an intellectual partnership must be possible within this relationship. We don't choose our children and they don't choose us but we can still foster many of these qualities in our relationship with them. *Trust* is the most important one. So, if you don't already, do what you say you will do when you say you will do it. Stick to agreements, commitments and promises the way you expect your child to.

Secondly, I had to decide when I would coach, lecture or mentor my son and make sure that I didn't mix these approaches when dealing with him. A coach is not a mentor. A good mentor is invaluable when one needs advice or insights into specific subjects. A coach often knows very little about what their client does and so does not give advice. You won't learn anything about your business from an executive coach. A good coach will get you thinking in new and interesting ways about your behaviour, your thinking and your potential. A lecturer is one who knows more than the student and can impart knowledge effectively.

You decide when to act as a lecturer, a mentor or a coach. There will be plenty of lecturers in our children's lives, lots of mentors too, but there will be very few true coaches. Of course, at times our knowledge and experience is invaluable and mentoring is the right thing to do. At other times our innate tendency to teach and lecture our offspring will drive us to do just that. Using the right modality at the right time will attract the least resistance from our children and the greatest behavioural impact.

Learning theory, research and our own experience tells us that lecturing is the least effective form of knowledge transfer. Think about the traditional university lectures or corporate trainings you've been subjected to over the years. Which were the most effective? I'm betting it was the programmes where you started out curious about the subject. Where the facilitator didn't list all the answers but helped you discover them for yourself. Where you were able to apply new concepts to your own experiences or even work hands on with new ideas. Am I right?

It wasn't the one where you bounced balloons around for an icebreaker and then sat listening to the lecturer sprout knowledge for two days from behind a lectern. These are the ones we forget. Our children are no different.

Remember that neither coaching, mentoring nor lecturing should define the relationship we have with our child. Once you have found the right mix between supporting your child as a coach and leading them as a mentor, try to stick to one approach at a time. If I start out coaching my son but get frustrated at his slow progress and switch to lecturing him, then he has little incentive to respond to a coaching approach next time around. It makes more sense for him to sit and wait for the inevitable lecture than engage me in a coaching conversation.

The Coaching Conversation

My son is physically small when compared to most boys his age.

He's not particularly sporty or boisterous on the playground either. Often, when he joins in rougher games he gets pushed around; on several occasions he also suffered at the hands and mind of a bully. His school is very proactive on bullying and physical abuse between children is not tolerated. So bullying takes different forms and is far more subtle than a shove or a punch. Verbal bullying, exclusion from games and other forms of emotional cruelty are dished out by children who don't yet understand the impact of their behaviour.

From about 6-years-old, there would be days when my son came home in tears, crying about the hurtful things some of the bigger boys had said to him on the bus. Initially I felt that he was being overly sensitive. I couldn't run to the teacher every time another child, boy or girl, called him a name. I also had no doubt that he was doing some name calling himself.

Reacting to this and trying to solve every painful problem he brought home was not going to help him. If anything, it would disempower him. I couldn't mentor him on how to deal with this either because I had no experience with bullying myself (I was not a small girl at school). Telling him not to react to the name calling would be harmful to his self esteem in the long run. Besides, it's hard not to react when stress hormones are coursing through your little body and you are so angry you want to lash out. He needed more than a cuddle from mommy; he needed a system for dealing with this, both during the event and afterwards. A way of making him feel OK about it that didn't deplete his ego. The coach in me got to work.

As he sat in the rocking chair in my study, in a reasonable mood,

I mentioned the last incident of verbal bullying on the school bus. He had been pushed to the point of swearing at a more senior child. Unfortunately, he was louder than the older boy and so was sent to the headmaster's office for his bad language. Instead of rehashing the just-tell-me-what-happened conversation, we explored his actions, reactions and feelings through a series of questions. At no point did I judge him or try to solve the problem for him.

My goal was to get him thinking through his own actions and understanding that he is not powerless in interactions with bigger kids – he just has to be smarter. Here is the coaching–style discussion that followed.

Q: Hun, how did you feel about what the boy said to you?
A: Very angry.
Q: So he called you a baby? Is it true, are you a baby?
A: No.
Q: Why did it make you angry then, if you know it's not true?
A: Because everyone else heard him say it.
Q: Could you have stopped him from saying it?
A: No.
Q: Do you think you reacted in the right way?
A: No, but I didn't know what else to say. I was so cross.
Q: What would you have liked to do differently?
A: To say something that makes me sound cool rather. And that won't get me into trouble.
Q: OK, so you want a line that you can say when you get angry, that sounds really cool but can't get you in trouble?

A: Yes. But what?

Q: Well, you tell me. What can you say every time someone calls you a name? Something that you won't forget and can use in different situations?

I asked him to go and think about what he could say next time he was in this position. He wanted to come up with something that sounded smart but would also let the "bully" know that he couldn't get to him. Of course I had several answers and nifty catch phrases ready to go (I'm a writer after all), but this was something he needed to own. So I bit my tongue and waited for his response.

His first few suggestions weren't going to cut it so I asked, "Mmm, is that the best you can do? Would that line always work?" Followed by, "Perhaps you'd remember something shorter more easily?" After a few tries he came up with a great suggestion that he still uses today (three years later). He says, "You may *think* that I'm a (nerd, baby, etc) but that doesn't make me one." If he's really angry or doesn't have time to think or centre himself, he simply takes a deep breath and says, "Well, it's a good thing I don't care what *you* think."

It takes real courage for a small boy to say this to anyone who is overpowering him with words. So we practiced it, out loud, several times at home. Now he can say it without thinking about it. The best consequence has been that the verbal bullying is affecting him less and less and, increasingly, he really doesn't care what they think of him.

4.2

A COACHING TOOL FOR BETTER DECISION MAKING

Sir John Whitmore is largely considered the granddaddy of executive coaching. He started out as a racing driver, a very good one, then became a sports psychologist and later translated trackside learnings into leadership and motivational tools in the very earliest days of executive coaching. As a father himself, he used what he had learnt in the field of performance coaching to make his life as a parent a little easier and more effective, reminding us that children who grow up thinking about the situations they find themselves in and the choices that they have within those situations are much more capable of making good decisions later on.[1] I'm betting that parents of teenagers the world over would all love for their offspring to make the most sensible decisions they can.

Sir Whitmore advises that the sooner we start allowing our children to make their own decisions, the sooner they will develop a database of consequences – causes and effects based on their choices. Of course we aren't going to let our toddler decide what to eat every night or what time to go to bed.

---

1   *Coaching and the GROW Model for Parents*, an interview with Sir John Whitmore hosted by Alan E. Wilson. Retrieved from YouTube on November 6, 2011.

However, there are situations where we can allow children as young as five to decide something for themselves and then deal with whatever consequence results from their own decision in a safe and supported environment. Start with the easy stuff: Do you want to wear the red or blue sweater today? Corn or potatoes for dinner? Half an hour of English or maths homework on Saturday before tennis? Do you want to invite Jean or Enrique to your party? Early choices teach them that they have an influence over their world and that their preferences matter and have consequences. As they get a little older (and perhaps a bit more stubborn), the decision-making process will take a bit more of your time and patience.

More Coaching Questions

Let's say it's really cold out and your daughter, Anna, wants to wear a fairy dress with no sweater or gloves or boots. Fine. You have a few options:

1. Tell her she doesn't go out unless she dresses warmly enough.
2. Help her make the right decision now and, hopefully, never have to deal with the issue again. Start by drawing her attention to the consequences of her decision making through questioning as we saw earlier.

Here are some ideas:

- Anna, honey, open the window and tell me if it's cold outside.
- If we let your little brother out into the freezing cold with only

his diaper on, would he get really cold and really sick?

- Would I be a good mommy if I let *you* get really cold and really sick?
- If you did get cold and sick, wouldn't you miss ballet class on Tuesday?
- If you went outside you'd get so cold that you'd have to come back inside all alone and miss out on playing with Emma.

How would that make Emma feel?

Honestly, I can go on and on with similar questions. Depending on your child, you'll only need to use one or two but be prepared to go on for a bit in the beginning if you have a stubborn tot or preteen. I use them all the time and now that my son is a bit older, he has started asking himself coaching questions. This is the ultimate goal of coaching – to have the coachee coach himself. As your child grows up, he will be much more comfortable devising his own options and then deciding between them without your help.

As you can see, you don't have to have a coaching qualification to do any of this effectively. Simply step back from the issue and engage your child through dialogue and questioning. Yes, it takes longer and takes your time away from work and your own challenges. However, if you stop telling your child what to do and ask questions to get to the root of the matter instead, you'll empower them to find their own solutions. Eventually, they'll start asking questions and thinking for themselves and all your efforts will pay off.

The GROW Coaching Model for Older Children

Here's another way to flex your coaching muscles: school reports. Your child's report card may show poor, average, above average or outstanding results. You're expected to comment, to praise and point out areas of improvement. Maybe even threaten to reduce pocket money or the opposite. Either way, report season can be a very stressful time for children and parents alike. How about not commenting on their grades initially? Ask your child to evaluate her school report herself: write down what she thought of her own performance and note the areas where she wants to improve, specifying how she is going to do so. The GROW coaching model is designed to do just this.

This is Whitmore's earliest coaching model and still a staple in coaching conversations. It's mainly used as a tool to help adults understand, plan and achieve their goals but can also be used as a nifty shortcut with our kids to help them think through their current reality, plan their next steps and so increase the likelihood of attaining their goals.

GROW is an acronym for:

G: Goal

What is it you want? Better grades overall, improvements in specific areas or simply to maintain current grades? Be very sure this is what your child wants and not what *you* really want, mom or dad.

R: Resources and reality

What do you have now to help you get it? What is standing in your way? Are there internal obstacles like lack of confidence? Or external such as lack of time, understanding or support?

O: Options

What options are available to you? Tutors? Playing less sport to free up more time for homework? More effective revising with a study plan? Not having a mobile phone in the room when doing homework?

W: Will or way forward

What will you do and how will you do it? Your role is to guide the creation of your child's action plan. Are his goals reasonable? Is he over or under confident in his ability? Can you help with extra tuition if he needs it?

Simply stating that, "I want to improve my marks by a grade," is not helpful at all. Rewarding your child on a final grade improvement at year end is also not helpful. Rewarding her for taking small actions towards her ultimate goal every day is where you want to be. Base incentives on how well she meets her own incremental targets, like doing an extra hour of maths on a Sunday.

Suddenly your child is responsible for her own success. This works from about 10-years-old when your child is able to reason and imagine the future and put their thoughts down on paper. They can even record their action plan on video and watch it at regular intervals or update it as they progress.

As my son gets older, my tactics will evolve to meet more mature challenges. He knows I will always look to him to think about how he can handle situations before I lecture him on how I would do it. I'm proud to be a parent coach. I coach my little boy with the exact same skills that I use with CEOs of multinational companies wrestling with multimillion-dollar challenges. It works. Mostly because my son is learning that through our dialogue, he can think of ways to solve his own problems and soon he'll be able to coach himself on more complex issues. He is already encouraging his friends to stop and think of alternative approaches before they react to tricky situations in the playground.

4.3

LISTENING TO
IGNITE THINKING

After supervisors in a manufacturing plant received training in emotional competencies such as how to listen better and help employees resolve problems on their own, lost-time accidents were reduced by 50%, formal grievances were reduced from an average of 15 per year to 3 per year, and the plant exceeded productivity goals by $250,000.

~ *The New Look in Behavior Modeling*, July 1996[1]

I first heard the term *generative attention* at a coaching conference. It was explained as *listening to ignite someone's thinking*. I was intrigued and invited the speaker to be interviewed for my YouTube Channel[2] and as part of my PhD research. Linda Aspey[3] happily joined me and we chatted further about listening and the pivotal role that it plays in successful coaching outcomes. In fact, she believes that providing a space where a client can

---

1 Pesuric, A., and Byham, W. (1996, July). *The New Look in Behavior Modeling*. Training and Development.

2 Coaching Club TV at www.youtube.com/c/TheCoachingClub

3 Linda Aspey is the Founder of Coaching for Leaders and an executive coach and consultant. She is a global faculty member of Nancy Kline's Thinking Environment. See www.coachingforleaders.co.uk

focus on their own thoughts, *without any interruption at all*, is the single most important component of a coaching conversation.

Other coaching qualities also come into play, such as being easeful, paying attention and asking insightful questions – but only when questions are invited by the client.[4] Imagine having one full hour where you are allowed to talk, think and mull over your own thoughts as much as you want without ever being interrupted, unless you specifically ask for a question or allow for further information. How interesting and liberating.

None of us welcome or enjoy being interrupted when we are talking but very few of us are completely innocent of interrupting others. For most of us, it's easy to interrupt our children because they have grown up with us doing just that. Many children expect that of their parents. We know what they are about to say and so we interrupt them, we've heard it before and so we interrupt them, we find a mistake in their reasoning and so we interrupt them, we disagree with them and so we interrupt them and so on and so on.

If we didn't interrupt them, what would we be doing? Listening. Coaches take listening to the next level. We listen for clues to our clients' true thoughts, inconsistencies in beliefs, biases in reasoning, blind spots and, of course, for the correct moment to interrupt them! But what if we didn't, what if we just listened with ease and attention to ignite their thinking?

There are many ways to listen. The three most common approaches can be described in terms of going to battle:

1. **Aggressive (listening to win the war)**: Listening for the points where a fellow speaker is wrong. Then, when you have

---

4   See www.timetothink.com/thinking-environment/ for more information on the "Ten Components of the Thinking Environment" by Nancy Kline.

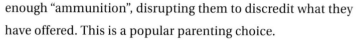

enough "ammunition", disrupting them to discredit what they have offered. This is a popular parenting choice.

2. **Defensive (listening not to lose a battle)**: Listening for those points on which you feel you are entitled to defend yourself or have been wronged. Then remembering those points and listening for the moment that you can jump in and offer your defence. This is a default listening style for most of us.

3. **Constructive (listening to find common ground and move forward)**: Listening for areas of agreement as a starting point to move forward from. Even if it is a point such as, "Can we both agree that you missed your curfew last night?"

What if we listened with no agenda? Just listened in order to hear what someone has to say? I used to wonder what the point of such an exercise would be. Why would I do that? Why would I just let someone ramble on and on? Then I realised that I was missing the point entirely because there really is no other point except to hear what someone has to say – because when someone feels heard, they feel valued. They are also far more likely to listen in return.

Something really interesting happens when someone hears their own thoughts out loud. They are able to evaluate themselves and hear if what they are saying makes any sense. Does your child really listen to you? When did you last truly pay attention to your child without interrupting, without correcting?

Of course, there will be times when your child's thinking reflects their lack of experience with the world and this is where you nudge them, through coaching or mentoring, to take on more thoughtful perspectives. Remember, we don't expect our children to have all the answers yet, but we won't know what they are thinking or where their thoughts will take them unless we can listen with no specific agenda.

It's important to note that listening to a child doesn't necessarily entail agreeing with what they are saying, but merely hearing them out completely so that you know where their thoughts are heading and can help them with it, and most importantly, so that they feel heard. Certainly, by the time your child reaches their teens you can't expect them to confide in you if they don't feel listened to by you.

TIPS AND TAKEAWAYS FROM CHAPTER 4

1. As a parent you can choose to lecture, mentor or coach your child through challenging situations. Coaching is the hardest and most time consuming initially, but pays off handsomely as your child learns to self-coach.

2. The earlier you allow your child to start making decisions, the more practice they will have at understanding cause and effect. This will help them make better decisions as their choices get harder and your ability to influence their thinking decreases.

3. Decision making is a process. Using a coaching model such as the GROW coaching model helps your child structure their decision making, understand their choices more clearly and think through the consequences of each.

5.1

BRAIN BUILDING BASICS

When you struggle to learn something, your
brain actually grows.

~ **Tweet by Bill Gates, August 2014**

Every child born today has access to a superpower that wasn't
available to any other generation. No, it's not an iPad or a Twitter
feed, it's access to knowledge about themselves: insight into their
own body, how it's built, sustained and degenerated. In particular,
how their mental and emotional circuitry work. I realise it sounds
a lot more like a biology assignment than a superpower, but
remember, even Superman had to learn how to use his gifts – to
fly straight, control his heat vision and not be disturbed by his
supersensitive hearing. Unlike us, he didn't have a manual on
how to do any of this. Thanks to cognitive neuroscience and
technological magic, you have access to information and tools
to help your budding superhero understand her mental and
emotional capabilities better than ever before.

Unsurprisingly, this is a popular and fast-growing area of

research and we are learning new things that impress the hell out of us almost every day. We don't know everything; in fact, we know less about ourselves than about our planet, but we do know that each one of us is an incredible feat of biological engineering and evolution. Our original cognitive specifications allowed us to navigate and survive in the more rural and informal settings of ancient jungles, forests and plains at a time when we were fair game on the food chain. Fast forward to now and we find ourselves in an environment that has changed faster than we have – we are still hosted in a body whose primary purpose remains to protect itself, survive and reproduce.

Whilst most of us are pretty adept at staying alive and reproducing, this ancient inbuilt circuitry of ours runs interference in our behaviour and decision-making ability when we least expect it. Higher-order thinking is a fairly recent phenomenon in human evolution. Our free-ranging ancestors had far less need for executive functions such as planning and decision-making skills generated by a well-developed prefrontal cortex[1] (the part of your brain that sits behind your forehead), so their brains looked very different to ours and so did their foreheads, which were teeny tiny in comparison, as you can see below.

1. Australopithecus robustus (between 2.0 and 1.2 million years ago)

2. Homo habilis

3. Homo erectus

4. Homo neanderthalensis

5. Homo sapiens (that's us and we appeared on the scene about 200,000 years ago)

---

1   The prefrontal cortex brain region is the seat of executive function overseeing our ability to plan, express ourselves, make decisions, imagine different outcomes, use moral judgement and moderate our behaviour.

Over the last 2 million years or so, evolution has literally pimped our brains and added processing power through complex connections that we don't yet fully understand. Yet the instinct-driven hindbrain of our ancestors didn't disappear as we grew more sophisticated. It's still there, just well hidden below layers of enlightenment.

To fully exploit the phenomenal tool tucked in our head, not only do we have to learn to exploit the higher-order thinking capacity of our more evolved prefrontal cortex, but we also have to right-size the influence that our basic programming still has on our thoughts and actions. This is certainly a reason that the field of emotional intelligence is booming. Perhaps this is the next evolutionary upgrade that is occurring across generations right now? As we use our emotional circuitry in new ways, such as through practising mindfulness, for example, new physical pathways will grow and change the layout of the brain over thousands of years.

But I'm getting ahead of myself. I get all fired up when I have an opportunity to help people understand their brain and hence, themselves, better. Most folk I meet in the corporate world don't know how their brain works and I can't help but think, "You carry around the most powerful operating system in the world right inside you and you don't know how to use it?" Most people know how to operate their smart phones better than they know how to use their own brains. So, if this is you too, and you want to raise your child as a thinker, I guess we need to start at the very beginning.

Basic Brain Building

It helps to think of the brain's basic wiring as a circuit board, just like the ones you built in your school's science lab, way back when. You had copper wires laid out in series or parallel circuits and then some type of switch or circuit breaker. When the switch was in the on position, the circuit was complete and current could flow and light up your light bulb or turn the little motor that was part of the circuit. When in the off position, your circuit was broken with a physical gap that stopped the current from flowing. In the brain, these switches are called synapses – connections that allow chemicals to flow across neurons and turn the circuit on. The more they are used, the easier it becomes for that circuit to fire. Use them enough and we create a memory that we can call on again and again. This is learning.

Neurons are the cells that sit on either side of the "switch" or synapse. They connect to each other via these synapses and form neural networks like information pathways across the brain. The more they exchange information, the thicker and stronger the connections get, until the pathway becomes a superhighway. Should a connection not receive stimulation, it will eventually lose its ability to connect to other neurons and disappear from the circuit board over time. Use it or lose it, literally.

At birth, babies' brains are already packed with almost all of the neurons they will need for their lives – more than 100 billion – three times as many stars as there are in the Milky Way. Every time I read that I can't help but think, "Wow, that's incredible." The first areas of the brain to develop are those that govern your baby's automatic bodily functions – as you know, they can scream and suck and coo straight out of the womb because the neural connections that govern these functions were created and strengthened in utero. Higher-order functions that emanate from the cerebral cortex, such as imagination and knowing right from wrong, aren't yet developed.

Even though the neurons of the brain already exist at birth, those that regulate emotions, generate higher-order thinking, language and abstract thought can't grow and develop till they are actually put into use through interaction with external stimuli after birth. They are also the last part of the brain to mature and will continue to grow into your child's early adult years. How much control do you think you have over how your child's brain grows and develops? I hope you answered, "More than I can imagine!"

> The growth in each region of the brain depends on receiving stimulation, which spurs activity and growth in that region.
>
> ~ **Child Welfare Information Gateway**

Once out of the snug but relatively dull murkiness of the womb, synapses occur in response to the young brain's experiences. Experiences that you control initially. Up to 2 million synapses per second fire through your baby's cognitive circuits. No wonder babies have to sleep so much – their brains are working incredibly hard every waking second and even when they sleep. But not all of these synapses, or connections, will be strengthened through repeated experience and about half of them will be lost before adolescence. The key here is to make sure that the right ones stick around and the unhelpful ones are pruned and lost forever. Whichever brain pathway is stimulated through experience will physically grow in response to that stimulation. For example, continuously talking to our babies will repeatedly fire language neurons and create connections in that area that become fairly stable memories over time. These language memories form a very important foundation for most other aspects of higher-order learning.

In the same way, if a child has suffered abuse as an infant, his fear pathways will be overly stimulated in response to his environment. An overly-developed response to fear creates hypersensitivity to perceived threats. If this persists for long enough, this sensitivity is likely to remain even after the child is brought into a loving environment. Many foster and adoptive parents experience the heartbreaking situation where a child can remain fearful of caregivers long after the abusive caregivers are replaced by loving ones. In such cases, stimulation to the child's regions of complex thought and emotional management would have been reduced in favour of the more primal survival pathways. If neglect persists for long enough, learning can be permanently impaired.

> While these children are often labelled as
> learning disabled, the reality is that their brains
> have developed so that they are constantly alert
> and are unable to achieve the relative calm
> necessary for learning.
>
> ~ **Child Trauma Academy**

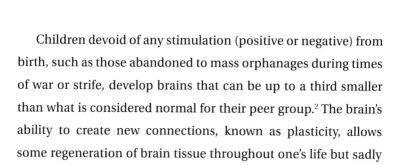

Children devoid of any stimulation (positive or negative) from birth, such as those abandoned to mass orphanages during times of war or strife, develop brains that can be up to a third smaller than what is considered normal for their peer group.[2] The brain's ability to create new connections, known as plasticity, allows some regeneration of brain tissue throughout one's life but sadly not to the extent that could guarantee a return to normal brain function for these children.

On the other hand, the smartest among us have the best wiring on their cognitive circuit boards. Science tells us that the brain volume a child achieves by the end of their first year plays a role in later intelligence.[3] Bigger brains result from more connections, remember? This allows messages to travel faster between different parts of the brain,[4] increasing memory and processing speeds. And how do we get stronger, faster connections between neurons in the brain?

We do some fun, basic brain building with our little ones.

2   A study led by Bruce D. and Perry, M.D., PhD., 2002, available at www.childtrauma.org
3   Catharine R. Gale, PhD, Finbar J. O'Callaghan, PhD, Maria Bredow, MBChB, Christopher N. Martyn, DPhil. (2006, October 4). *The Influence of Head Growth in Foetal Life, Infancy, and Childhood on Intelligence at the Ages of 4 and 8 Years.* PEDIATRICS Vol. 118.
4   Professor Ed Bullmore, Professor of Psychiatry at Cambridge, specialising in brain imaging. In his research, he measured the efficiency with which different parts of the brain communicated with each other and found that high integration of brain networks seems to be associated with high IQ. Find him at the Cambridge Neuroscience Department (www. neuroscience.cam.ac.uk/directory/profile.php?etb23).

5.2

BASIC BRAIN-BUILDING EXERCISES FOR INFANTS AND TODDLERS

Let's recap on what we know so far. Baby's brains are amazing. All brains are amazing. Brain growth in each functional area is determined by receiving repetitive external stimulation. The type of stimulation determines which connections in the brain are used and so which areas of the brain develop. Genes play a part in determining the layout of the circuitry in the brain and developmental potentials. Which circuits are completed and expressed is determined again, by experience. Oh, and did I mention that once your child has built up sufficient networks of good strong synapses in the areas of her brain that support memory, language and higher cognitive functions, then learning in general becomes easier because the learning pathways are wide open? Neat, isn't it?

Your Child's Developmental Blueprints

Brain building is much like building a large city from scratch. Skyscrapers can't go up until foundations are laid. Foundations won't be laid until subterranean sewage and electrical pipes are in place. We can't learn language until memory pathways are ready, for example. We can't comprehend shapes until we can manipulate objects. There are very specific ages when certain pathways are laid down for the first time and also when they are ready to be strengthened.

Motor development, vision and language pathways are first wired from birth to 2-years-old while social development and emotional intelligence pathways are laid down between 0- to 48-months-old.[1]

As you can see, important foundations are laid in the first two years before your child even goes to kindergarten. So before we talk about different types of intelligence, here are some ways to spend quality time with your infant that will strengthen their learning pathways and enhance foundational brain growth. If you no longer have an infant and don't plan on having another one in the future, then skip right over to Chapter 6 on fluid intelligence.

Language Development

Your child's first year is all about sounds. Talk, talk, talk to your child, face to face. Your child will hear sounds from the TV and from around him, but he needs to see your mouth moving and the body language that goes with the sound in order to catalogue words correctly. Of course your infant will be most engaged when you are close enough to make eye contact (remember your baby is short-sighted for the first few months). Keep sentences short and repeat important ideas with all the sound effects you can muster.

---

1   Schiller, P. (2010) *Early Brain Development Research Review and Update.* EXCHANGE Magazine, Nov/Dec 2010 edition.

Try this: What's in the box?

Introduce your baby to a new object that you pick out of a box or from under a cloth. Ordinary objects are best, like a wooden spoon, a book or a pair of socks. Hold it up and ask, "What's this?" Then let your child explore it – either let them grasp it or turn it around slowly so that they can see all of it. Describe it as you go. When he's had a good look, tell him what it is and show him how it's used.

In your baby's second year, the brain's language centre evolves dramatically as synaptic activity increases. Vocabulary expands exponentially, but only if they are exposed to many words and things to name. Pull "known" objects out of the box, ask what they are and let your toddler tell you what they know and help them with what they don't. Then give him cuddles for being so smart.

Starting Kindergarten Soon?

At around 8-months-old, your baby's conscious memory stabilises. He begins to understand that objects can exist even when he can't see them because now he can remember them. Your baby can look at a partially-hidden toy and know what it is because he has a complete image stored in his memory. This is when stranger anxiety can begin because a stranger is someone they don't already have a mental image of. Visiting new places may have the same effect on your toddler as new faces do.

If you are worried about your little one's first day at kindergarten – I've not met a first-time parent who isn't – you can use what you know about memory to ease their first day anxiety – and yours.

Start by building up memories of the kindergarten. Look at

the school's website, explain the different pictures they have on it. Print out the picture of their new teacher and let them look at it often. If you live nearby, try to walk past the school and point out the different things in the playground and how much fun the other kids are having. Do this until they have fairly stable memories of the school and the playground before they even get there. Talk to them about feeling scared and how they can cope without you. Use your new parent-coaching skills to talk them through different scenarios and allow them to think of ways they can help themself, until they feel brave enough to go it alone.

Foundations of Focus and Mental Scaffolding

Is your little girl reaching for a toy that is just outside of her reach? Your first instinct is to pick it up and give it to her, right? This is what I used to do, for sure, and still want to do when I can see that my son can't reach his Lego Black Pearl on the top of his bookshelf or can't find the DVD that I asked him to pack away a week ago. But I stop myself because now I know that this is both a behavioural and cognitive learning opportunity.

Scaffolding happens when you follow your child's lead in activities that they initiate. You provide just enough support to challenge her to the next level without overwhelming her with frustration. So nudge the toy to just within her reach. She still has to try to get what she wants – which requires both determination and focus – but she is learning that she can help herself, that this requires effort and that daddy won't just hand her whatever she wants when she wants it. She is also experiencing the triumph of achievement. Don't rob her of that.

As you can see, these are not formal sit-down-and-learn exercises. Goodness knows your child will have enough of those throughout their lifetime. For many of us, the time that we spend with our children is limited to those precious minutes and hours that we carve out in the evenings and over weekends to be nothing but a father or a mother. My son's days are as packed as mine – crowded with homework and sport, parties, concerts and extra maths. Do I really want to take up our time together with critical-thinking tutoring delivered by moi? Absolutely not, which is why the activities I suggest are ones that can be used in everyday interactions with your school-going children, such as going shopping, parking the car or talking about a birthday party. Consider these exercises impromptu pop-up training for the school of life. Like any exercise routine, if these conversations don't fit in with your life, aren't fun and don't eventually produce results, you will drop them and be reluctant to try again. The next chapter discusses more brain-building activities as we look at working memory as a building block of *fluid intelligence* (remember fluid or raw intelligence as a quality of a hyper-skilled employee, as introduced in Chapter 2?).

Further references and resources

- Ramey, C. T. & Ramey, S. L. (1999). *Right from Birth: Building your Child's Foundation for Life: Birth to 18 Months.* Goddard parenting guides. New York: Goddard Press
- Schiller, P. (1999). *Start Smart!: Building Brain Power in the Early Years.* Beltsville, MD: Gryphon House
- Calvin, W. (1996). *How Brains Think: Evolving Intelligence Then and Now.* New York: Basic Books
- Sylwester, R. (1995). *A Celebration of Neurons: An Educator's Guide to the Human Brain.* Association for Supervision & Curriculum Development.

TIPS AND TAKEAWAYS FROM CHAPTER 5

1. A young brain grows and learns through exposure to different stimuli. You choose what to expose your infant to and how much to interact with them – so make it count.

2. Brain growth achieved in the first year will influence later attainment levels.

3. Language and memory develop rapidly in the toddler years – play games with your little one to boost these pathways in the brain.

4. Speak to your baby as much and as clearly as you can, about anything. This may mean putting your phone away when walking with her in the park, at a restaurant or when grabbing a quick coffee at Starbucks with her in tow.

INTERLUDE

When basking in the latest cognitive research and cool stuff that we didn't know yesterday, it may be tempting to think that the problems we face in preparing our children for life are new world problems unique to our generation. But what if they aren't? What if we've been trying to solve the same problems for decades using the same thinking that created them in the first place? What if, today, we merely have a better lexicon of terms to voice our concerns and insights?

In the early 1940s, the war effort in the US required a certain standard of literacy amongst army recruits. To achieve this, disparate schools across the nation were required to conform to a standard curriculum for the first time. This was the beginning of a revolution that also severed the connection between wealth and access to education in the US. By 1947, standardised testing was introduced and became the only way to gain admission into higher education.

Assistant superintendent of Cincinnati Public Schools at the time, George H. Reavis, was part of this transition. Perhaps because of or in response to it, he penned and published a fable in the early 1940s that reflected his view of the changes around him. Remember that this was a time still untroubled by a deep-seated scholastic status quo and a tipping point where the decisions of a few changed the lives of almost everyone.

Now who doesn't love a fable in the middle of a book on thinking about thinking? It's been around for more than 70 years but still rings clear and true for many today.

The Animal School By George H. Reavis

Once upon a time, the animals decided they must do something heroic to meet the problems of "a new world". So they organized a school. They adopted an activity curriculum consisting of running, climbing, swimming and flying. To make it easier to administer the curriculum, all the animals took all the subjects.

The duck was excellent in swimming, in fact better than his instructor, but he made only passing grades in flying and was very poor in running. Since he was slow in running, he had to stay after school and also drop swimming in order to practice running. This was kept up until his webbed feet were badly worn and he was only average in swimming. But average was acceptable in school, so nobody worried about that except the duck.

The rabbit started at the top of the class in running, but had a nervous breakdown because of so much make-up work in swimming. The squirrel was excellent in climbing until he developed frustration in the flying class where his teacher made him start from the ground up instead of from the treetop down. He also developed a "charlie horse" from overexertion and then got a "C" in climbing and a "D" in running.

The eagle was a problem child and was disciplined severely. In the climbing class he beat all the others to the top of the tree, but insisted on using his own way to get there.

At the end of the year, an abnormal eel that could swim exceedingly well, and also run, climb and fly a little, had the highest average and was valedictorian.

The prairie dogs stayed out of school and fought the tax levy because the administration would not add digging and burrowing to the curriculum. They apprenticed their children to a badger and later joined the groundhogs and gophers to start a successful private school.

6.1

THE SECRETS OF RAW INTELLIGENCE

I teach a humanities subject in an "outstanding" sixth-form college in an affluent area. My students are bright, engaged and well-behaved, but there is something missing: they cannot think. They treat education like a military exercise. Students think there are set answers to life's questions; they want a formula for the number of sentences per paragraph and expect information they can rote-learn. How does this prepare them for anything? A book is a decoration, a door-stop, a paperweight. An idea is irrelevant. A thought is a distraction.

~ *The Guardian*, The Secret Teacher, 7 February 2015

Adrian is a pink-cheeked 10-year-old with half-moon eyes and a mischievous smile that never seems to let up. When we met he was perched on a red beanbag in the library of his British international school surrounded by the week's space-themed projects. Planets dangled precariously in cardboard universes sporting styrofoam suns as shiny foil-clad spacecraft showed off the students' vision for space travel of the future. Adrian talks with remarkable confidence, easily telling me about his favourite things and teachers with words so sophisticated, I have to remind myself that I'm talking to a 10-year-old. "I'm rereading *20,000 Leagues Under The Sea*," he says, "because Captain Nemo is such an iconic character. He's kind, cruel and compelling all at the same time, not a typical Hollywood hero."

With a mind that insightful at this age, you'd imagine that Adrian was top of his class. When I asked him about the subjects he liked least, his attention turned to the patterns on the carpet beneath him. "Maths, I'd say. Because I am supposed to learn the times tables by heart, actually I should have done that two years ago in Year 3. I'm just not as quick as I should be with mental maths and my handwriting is still not good enough. It's too big and takes me too long to write stuff down. I have extra classes for maths and English and handwriting. Basically I don't get to go to the fun stuff like art because I'm always in an extra class – oh, and I do extra spelling too."

Adrian didn't really want to talk about maths or English or even Mandarin, what he really wanted to chat about was shopping trolleys. He was designing one for his mum. "I have to do groceries with her and she always complains about how hard it is to push the trolley," he says, "it sticks and skids and then doesn't stop when she wants it to. So I'm designing one with a small electric motor, gears on the steering and air brakes." Two weeks before, Adrian had designed a Pac-Man style game using a game-building app on a school iPad during ICT. It was loaded up to a game-sharing site and was already enjoying hundreds of downloads by preteens around the world.

His report cards show him to be an underperformer on almost all measures (except Mandarin and English Reading for which he was "average" then) but there is no way this boy is unintelligent. We discussed *his* view on dark matter – because I didn't have a view on the matter at all – and how the cosmos is expanding. In fact, I found him quicker, more curious and knowledgeable about the world than his "smarter" classmates whom I was able to chat to. I couldn't help but wonder if Adrian's scenario is behind so many successful college dropouts from Thomas Edison and Abraham Lincoln to Walt Disney, Steve Jobs and so many others.

All these iconic characters who never finished their studies at school or university have what is known as fluid, or raw, intelligence. If Adrian's school had a test for it, he would have been considered gifted. Instead, he lives with the label of "average". In 15 years' time though, he'll blow the socks off some lucky employer or venture capitalist. Hopefully by then he would have been able to prove himself with his own brand of smart or skip the corporate world entirely and make a living on his own terms.

Raw Intelligence

Like crude oil, silica or wheat flour, raw intelligence is unrefined and laced with potential. It's not intelligence about a specific subject but rather the ability to apply one's inbuilt thinking tools to both everyday and exceptional challenges. Like molten gold, it can be set into a shape, melted down again and remoulded into something new without losing its value. Doesn't this just sound like intelligence as traditionally measured in IQ tests? Yes, but mostly, no. The field of IQ testing is a vast sea of data fed by hundreds of rivers, each searching for the one defining source of our intelligence. It's a wonderfully turbulent and controversial ocean-sized field of study.

A question I'm often asked is, "Can I really change my child's intelligence?" It's a good question centred on a rather old-fashioned debate: are we born with a fixed level of intelligence or can intelligence be nurtured and increased, or decreased, depending on our environment? This is an ongoing discussion fuelled by research in neuroscience now rather than subjective testing and here is what we know so far.

Genetics lays down our intellectual circuitry or potential but our environment decides which of these circuits get activated and to what degree. Basic levels of intelligence are increasing with each new generation as educators become more effective at teaching and more children have access to schools and environments that nurture cognitive development. Schooling and other academic interventions increase objective measures of intelligence whilst long summer holidays do the opposite.

Is the intelligence as measured by traditional IQ tests the same as the raw intelligence that companies are looking for? Wouldn't it make every recruiter's job super easy if it were the same? "Forget your CV, just send in your IQ score sheet." Those with the highest IQ would be well bid for and offered starting salaries many times the average starting salary for graduates today. Everyone would know exactly what they're worth. We could even have a global pay scale based on IQ. Completely fair and transparent. How about that?

That wouldn't work for Adrian nor would it work for every company shaping the future. Do you remember the list of qualities that these employers are looking for in future leaders from Chapter 2? Adaptability, resilience, social, emotional and raw intelligence.

Raw intelligence fits squarely in the domain of the critical thinker. It represents our capacity to think logically and systematically in ways that allow us to solve problems independent of acquired knowledge. It encompasses the innate processes we use to find patterns or relationships in novel situations and create new solutions. It allows us to think bravely but cautiously and rally all our thinking tools, including working memory, around tricky problems or creative endeavours. Psychologists call this fluid intelligence.

On the other hand, acquired or learned knowledge is known as crystallised intelligence. It represents the stuff we know about through knowledge, skills and experience, or what we need to know to pass our maths or history exams. The Confucian heritage education model currently focuses on crystallised intelligence. The same is true of most aspects of the US and UK education curricula. As you can imagine, the relationship between these two types of smarts is a new, interesting and potentially controversial area of research.

The Bill and Melinda Gates Foundation and the US National Institute of Health were interested to know if students who improved their scores on standard school tests were also able to improve their fluid intelligence. Their well-credentialed research[1] showed that public (government-funded) schools in the US that were able to raise their student's test scores on standardised tests of crystallised intelligence were not able to replicate this improvement on tests of fluid intelligence. In short, doing well at school didn't lead to gains in cognitive skills. It would seem that fluid intelligence is not a bonus by-product of studying hard and being a good student. You suspected that already, right?

Make no mistake, the combination of declarative knowledge (crystallised intelligence) and fluid intelligence is very powerful. Having Lego blocks plus the ability to put them together in new and innovative ways is much more useful than owning an acre of Lego blocks but only being able to build something by following the step-by-step instruction booklet. Before we can help our little loved ones develop this seemingly precious skill, we should probably look at what fluid intelligence is.

You will find its definition as fluid as its substance with scientists and researchers continuing a century-old argument of what exactly makes us intelligent beyond knowledge. So far we have:

1. Working memory and processing speed
2. Adaptability, resilience and curiosity
3. Problem-solving skills

As we've already seen, these are also the skills most needed to supplement many school and higher-education curricula around

---

1   Trafton, A. (2013, December 11). *Even When Test Scores Go Up, Some Cognitive Abilities Don't*. Retrieved from news.mit.edu/2013/even-when-test-scores-go-up-some-cognitive-abilities-dont-1211.
      This study was a collaboration with the Center for Education Policy Research at Harvard University, Transforming Education, and Brown University, and was funded by the Bill and Melinda Gates Foundation and the National Institute of Health. MIT neuroscience professor John Gabrieli was the lead author.

the world with 2 and 3 also being high on recruiters' hit lists. Over the next few chapters, I'll chat about each one in turn and give you ideas to help your child foster these talents as they grow. After that, we'll jump straight into good decision making and nourishing creativity and innovation. Of course, this is all aimed squarely at helping your children be better thinkers, but if it also helps you rekindle your skills in these areas, then that's useful too.

6.2

PUTTING MEMORY TO WORK

Working memory is the unsung hero of intelligence, the part of our short-term memory that we call on for immediate perception, information and language processing. It can be compared to your computer's high-speed memory that stores data or bits of the programs that you are currently working on so that it can access them more quickly.

The size and processing speed of our working memory is closely tied to our ability to reason and solve problems. This nifty piece of kit processes and records verbal and visuospatial[1] information with the help of an executive system that controls how attention is allocated between these two information sources. As impressive as it sounds, scientists and users alike report two rather fundamental flaws in our working memory: it has very limited capacity and leaks like a colander.

Sometimes, when you ask your computer to process very demanding tasks, such as rendering an enormous image in Photoshop, or labouring away at a mammoth spreadsheet, it slows down and can even grind to a halt. At this point, it may

---

1   Relating to or denoting the visual perception of the spatial relationships of objects.

complain about having insufficient memory to complete the task. If you can't upgrade your computer's memory then there's nothing to do but sit and wait, and wait, for it to finish grinding away. Sometimes the process times out and you have to start again. In much the same way, if our brain's working memory is too small and too slow, similar problems will plague our thinking, without the ability to reboot and start again.

We can't simply add more storage space to our mental motherboard. You may have heard that we can only hold five to nine pieces of information in working memory. I used to dismiss this as an urban legend and insult to human intelligence, but I was wrong on all fronts. It would seem that us grownups can indeed only hold a limited amount of independent chunks of information in our working memory. Neither five nor nine is a big number but the difference between being able to work with five or with nine bits of data is like shopping in the UK property market with £500,000 or £900,000. The difference in what you can buy with these two amounts is vast – £500k would get you a two-bed flat in London whereas £900k might get you a four-bed semi-detached house. A larger working memory capacity means that more variables can be considered at the same time.

If you're curious to find out the size of your working memory, then try this: read through these numbers with the intention of remembering them: 39728456

(Bear with me, you'll see why in a bit.)

For children, working memory is used in almost all areas of cognition from answering questions in reading comprehension to contemplating different objects, words or numbers in order to group them or perform calculations. When working through a problem, especially word problems, assumptions and facts must be held in mind and considered together until conclusions can be deduced from them. In reading comprehension, new or ambivalent words must be retained in memory until their meaning can be gleaned from the remainder of the sentence or paragraph. You'll have noticed that these are not activities where your child is learning new knowledge such as the periodic table or the properties of isosceles triangles. Learning facts requires repetition to add the information to our long-term memory stores and top up our crystalline intelligence.

Given its size limitation, information stored in working memory must leak or decay to make way for new data. Ever walk to the fridge, get distracted en route and then forget what you came for as you peer at the starkly lit milk and marg? Yup, that's working memory in action and it brings me to the next important aspect of fluid intelligence, namely, processing speed. I can continue the analogy of a computer here but I think you probably get it already.

Faster processing speed means that we can complete our reasoning before the stored information decays. Processing speed is a global indicator and does not change between different tasks. The speed attained is proportional to age – for example a 12-year-old will process information at about half the speed of a young adult. This means that your 10-year-old will take longer to come up with a solution to a maths problem than you simply because he is processing at more than half the speed that you are. A child that is able to consider stored facts faster will have a better chance of using the information before it is pushed out by new facts than a child with the same-sized working memory but much slower processing speed.

Remember those numbers from earlier? Can you recall them?

Only a few?

That's not too bad.

Now try and remember them as chunks of larger numbers. Say them out loud if you can.

39	72	84	56
thirty-nine	seventy-two	eighty-four	fifty-six

We'll check on them again in a little while and see if your score improves.

So if working memory and processing speed are foundational in fluid intelligence, how can we help our children develop confidently in this area? Let's look at some fun things to do to with your little and not so little ones.

6.3

WORKING MEMORY BOOTCAMP

The strength of working memory depends on neuronal excitability in a distributed network of cortical regions as assessed by transcranial magnetic stimulation.[1] I can't pretend to love wading through endless academic research like this in my quest to help us all raise thinkers. If I were to translate this into human, I would say: the strength of our working memory depends on how strong and fast neurons fire across different areas of the brain. We already know that neurons get better and stronger through use. So here are some exercises that specifically improve the speed and capacity of working memory. For me, one of the most interesting discoveries about working memory is that physical activity of all kinds boosts its capacity and hence our fluid intelligence.

From working with executives, I know that the quality of new ideas and decision making around a boardroom table decreases significantly when participants have been on the road for a few days and unable to get their zumba, yogilates or soul cycle fix. Apart from all the other well-publicised benefits of exercise, growth[2] hormones are also released during sustained physical

---

1   Nathalie Schicktanz et al. (2013, November). *Motor Threshold Predicts Working Memory Performance in Healthy Humans.* University of Basel and University of Bern and the Center of Neurology and Neurorehabilitation, Luzerner Kantonsspital

2   Andrew S. Whiteman et al. (2013, December). *Aerobic Fitness and Hormones Predict Recognition Memory in Young Adults.* Boston University Medical Centre

activity. They won't make you taller but will benefit an area of the brain (the hippocampus) crucial for learning and memory, so aerobic fitness has been linked directly to improved brain health and memory capacity. We know how important exercise is for our body, so why shouldn't it be just as important for our brain? I'm sure I don't need to give you a list of exercises to do with your kids here. Just get them moving and grooving every day. Swap 20 minutes of Minecraft for boogie music and a spot of Wii Fit hula dancing before dinner or an old fashioned speed walk around the block, or even better, suit them up with a dust buster and furniture polish and let them help with the housework – it's all for a good cause.

Turn Memory On

If your child is still young enough for bedtime stories, then try this little mental exercise at bedtime tonight and tomorrow night. Read a bedtime story or chapters as usual and then have a little Q&A afterwards. Start with big open questions such as, "What did we learn about our main character tonight?" or, "Why did the mean girls not want to play with Anna?" Then get more specific such as, "How many children did Anna invite to her party?" Notice how fast and accurately your child is able to deliver answers. Of course *you'll* need to pay full attention as well. The following night, repeat the exercise with a different story. This time, before you start, tell your child to listen well because you'll ask her a few questions again at the end.

Unless your child is already a whizz at listening comprehension, you'll be surprised at how much better she will do on the second night. (Of course you'll be expecting it, but try acting surprised and pleased anyway.)

What led to such an improvement in your child's processing speed and accuracy? Well, it's not because you "practised" it the night before as the information is completely new and different. What you did differently this time is prime her working memory. You turned it on by telling her she will need to remember facts from the text *before* you read it to her. The brand new science[3] behind this shows us that memory has to be activated in order to remember even the simplest details after we've been exposed to them. Of course this is done either consciously (by telling ourselves to pay attention) or unconsciously (because we want to remember the info for later use).

Eyewitness testimony uses long-term memory and the ability to reconstruct fragments of information. Information that would have had to pass through working memory on the way in to long-term memory. For some time now, scientists have questioned the reliance on eyewitness testimony in criminal convictions. Their scepticism is duly supported with the results of DNA testing, which expose our inability to accurately record and recall information when we're not expecting to have to do so. In fact a staggering 73% of the 239 criminal convictions overturned in the US through DNA testing since it was introduced in the 1990s, were based on eyewitness testimony.[4] That's 174 innocent lives ruined by someone's perfectly normal memory.

Educators already know through experience that "curiosity" is the foundation of retention. What does this mean to us as parents? Well, if a child is curious about the subject they are learning,

---

3   Hui Chen and Brad Wyble. (2015, February). Amnesia for object attributes: failure to report attended information that had just reached conscious awareness. *Psychological Science*.

4   Arkowitz, H. and Lilienfeld, S.O. (2009, January 8). *Why science tells us not to rely on eyewitness accounts. Scientific American*.

learning and retention will be much higher. We'll talk a lot more about curiosity in innovation but right now it's important to know that a state of curiosity not only turns memory on but runs it at full capacity. My son can tell me exactly what date the Titanic sank and when several other man-made disasters occurred. Not because he's learnt them but because he's fascinated by this topic. He takes out library books and reads up on it simply because he wants to. He's curious and his general knowledge in this area is startling. If I were to ask him for the properties of a scalene triangle, he probably wouldn't be able to tell me because maths doesn't arouse his curiosity in the same way.

How can we make our kids curious about mundane, everyday topics like homework? Challenge them. If they're doing a project, challenge them to find some new and interesting fact, on their own, that will blow their classmates away. When learning for a test, challenge them to see how many mnemonics they can invent to help them remember the details. Be curious and ask them what their limits are and how they can exceed those.

Memory by Stealth

Remember that memory capacity is built through use – like all pathways in the brain. If you still have a toddler, why not take the "What's in the box?" game further by pulling a toy from under the cloth or the shoebox, asking your toddler what it is and then letting her describe it and give it a name. Perhaps she'll say, "It's a puppy dog bear and I'll call it Fuzzy Wuzzy Big Eyes." Do encourage crazy names just for fun and because they are easier to remember. Then, ask her to help you remember the name by reminding you just before bedtime. Again, reward with praise when you can see that she has held on to that piece of information for hours just so that she could help daddy or mommy remember Fuzzy Wuzzy Big Eyes.

Going to the grocery store? Get your toddler to remember one item from the list. Then a few months later, ask them to remember two items and so on. Pretend that you forgot what those items are and together you can try to remember if it was diapers or dummies that you were out of. Honesty, this is a good exercise to do all your life, as continuously forcing new connections in the brain will slow down cognitive ageing significantly.

Mnemonics are helpful to old and young memories, too. Did you park your car in Lot 27, Basement 2? The parking lots in Singapore are so large that I usually just note the location of my parking spot in my reminders app on my iPhone. That's just lazy thinking, isn't it? In order to test the usefulness of mnemonics for working memory, my son and I have started using them to help us remember our parking spaces and taxi numbers when we book a cab. So, Lot 27, Basement 2 would become 27 baboons in a B2 bomber, and we never forget where we parked anymore. Being able to visualise numbers is very important for mental maths and later, for systems thinking. Cab numbers here are four digits long, and two days ago I took a cab with the number 9034. Breaking these numbers up into 90 and 34 and then asking your child to see them in his head in big black, pink, blue with yellow-spotted figures will help them "see" and remember numbers.

Remember those numbers you looked at earlier? The ones I asked you to remember? Can you?

No, I'm not going to list them here, that wouldn't help you. I'm guessing that you remember more this time round than you did the first time? You probably know why, too. The second round of numbers was the same as the first but I chunked them into smaller chunks so you had only four instead of eight numbers to remember (39 instead of 3 and 9, etc.). That's a little easier on working memory, isn't it?

As part of my undergraduate degree, I learnt to program large relational CRM databases. Many years later and despite passing all my exams, I don't remember any aspect of the actual coding languages I used. I do remember many late, frustrating nights working on pieces of code with the mantra GIGO running through my head as I wrestled with boolean statements and unruly syntax. GIGO – garbage in, garbage out – a piece of code can only do what it is programmed to do and if it is programmed badly, it will do it badly. Our working memory is no different.

Even if our working memory is primed and ready to retain info for us, it can only remember what we pay attention to. It sounds kind of obvious, doesn't it? If our children can't settle down and pay attention to what's important, then no amount of critical-thinking training will change their outcomes. Learning to focus from a young age is so important that a baby can do it naturally. He focuses on your face when you speak, on an object when you show it to him or on the dog's tail the first time he sees it wag excitedly, to the exclusion of all else. Being short-sighted is actually very useful for concentration when you're just a little tot. But later your child's world explodes into a cornucopia of sights, sounds and fun stuff to do and be distracted by.

The popularity of practicing mindfulness is no doubt partly driven by a need to shut out the busyness around us. With its growing popularity and proven benefits, it was bound to find its way into the classroom. A very welcome trend indeed. It is being packaged as the WD40 of education. "Helping students find the focus needed to achieve their academic goals," says Katherine Weare, Emeritus Professor at the Universities of Exeter and Southampton's mood disorder centre, "The evidence is that kids' tests improve as a result and children who can sit and breathe for a few minutes before they start an exam will do better compared with those who don't." If it's going to help Johnny get the grade he wants then that's great, but what's really important here is that he's creating a habit of sustained concentration.

Playing with Lego blocks without a TV on for distraction, reading a book without the latest hip hop funk rock blaring in the background will do much the same for concentration levels. It's really about paying attention to how your child pays attention and the spaces where your child is expected to work on important tasks.

The speed and size of working memory are the hardware in our fluid intelligence system. Hardware does the physical processing work but software tells it what and how to process. The software of fluid intelligence is what we'll look at next.

TIPS AND TAKEAWAYS FROM CHAPTER 6

1. The size and processing speed of your child's working memory is closely tied to their ability to reason and solve problems.

2. Working memory gets sharper and stronger through priming, use and physical exercise.

3. From an early age, try building your child's working memory by stealth. Involve your children in daily activities such as remembering items on a shopping list, where you parked the car, etc.

4. Create areas where your child can learn, work or play that are distraction free. If they are building Lego, turn off the TV.

PART 3

SUCCESS SKILLS FOR THE JOURNEY OF LIFE

7.1

THINKING ABOUT THINKING

Three a.m.: he lay awake again. The same noises shuffled in from the lawn; formless noises like footsteps and whispers or wind and softly groaning trees. Every day that week on his way to work, he had noticed the same bearded man standing on the corner near the station café, behind dark sunglasses that seemed to track his progress across the platform. He wondered if he was being followed as he passed the newsstand where headlines flashed the trauma of at least 200 people killed and thousands injured in a terrorist bombing in Madrid – Spain's own 9/11. At first he thought he was simply being paranoid. Had helping a Taliban supporter in a custody battle over a year ago come back to haunt him? Four a.m.: more muffled voices in the yard. Every day he grew more certain that he was being watched. Doors that were open when his wife left home were locked when she returned. Small things were out of place in the house, in his bathroom. He prayed to Allah that his family would be safe. After all, he had done nothing wrong and had nothing to fear.

This is the position Brandon Mayfield was in on 6 May 2014

when two FBI agents knocked on the door of his law office in Portland, Oregon. At first they were polite, just wanting to ask him a few questions, but as they eventually forced their way through the door under cover of a warrant for his arrest, Brandon knew something more serious was going on – really serious. He soon learnt that his fingerprint had been found on a bag of detonators near the scene of the terrorist bombings in Spain. The print was a near perfect match.

Mayfield had converted to Islam to marry his Egyptian wife, Mona. He had defended a convicted terrorist in a child custody case, giving him known links to a terrorist organisation. His computer held further "evidence" against him in the form of searches for "flights to Spain" and "flying lessons". In addition, he'd received combat training during his time in the US military. Surely Mayfield was a terrorist and the FBI had their man?

Brandon Mayfield was a lawyer and a father of four who gave his time and expertise to help those who couldn't afford high legal fees. His passport had long since expired and he hadn't left the US in over 10 years. Despite this, the FBI had a solid case against him with only the opinion of an independent forensic expert outstanding. This expert was brought in to verify the FBI's findings and his verdict would largely seal Mayfield's fate. Surely this man would find the error in the FBI's analysis, surely this was all a huge mistake? Unfortunately, the forensic expert also decreed with certainty that the print on the bag in Spain was indeed that of the accused. "100% Verified" declared the FBI report. The full weight of the justice system now pinned Mayfield to the wall, yet he maintained he was wrongfully accused.

The Spanish government wasn't so sure. After Mayfield had been in captivity for two weeks, it emerged that the Spanish police had repeatedly informed the FBI that they had found another match for the print on the detonator bag – an Algerian national. Their suspect had a credible motive and had actually been in Spain at the time. Given this new information, the FBI was obliged to release Mayfield.

How Could the FBI Have Been So Wrong?

Former CIA employee, contractor to the NSA and whistle-blower, Edward Snowden, has publicly spoken out against the dangers of mass surveillance[1] for both ethical and practical reasons. An enormous pond of stagnant data allows anyone with the necessary clearance to retroactively mine pieces of information, pick out the ones that confirm the theory of the day and create a plausible story to back it up. In other words, reshaping the puzzle piece to fit the hole in the puzzle. The Mayfield case is particularly striking because of the number of "experts" convinced of his guilt despite the lack of any concrete evidence. It seems that there was enough information available for these officials to pick the facts that fitted the case against him. They suffered from a rather public case of *confirmation bias* aided and abetted by the number of "facts" available to them. The results showed that their thinking tools weren't as sharp and well-calibrated as they should have been. Thankfully, the Spanish police acted as a counterbalance in this case, but what about the many cases where the decision of a single agency, group or even person is relied upon?

What does any of this have to do with your child? As always, let's start with what this has to do with you.

1   From Edward Snowden's recorded message to the National Union of Journalists (NUJ, UK and Ireland) and International Federation of Journalists (IFJ) conference – Journalism in the Age of Mass Surveillance: Safeguarding Journalists and their Sources. Hosted by Guardian News & Media. London, October 16, 2014.

Thinking Tools

No matter what you do for a living, your past, present and future result from a collection of small and large decisions strung together across time and circumstance, incorporating varying measures of random events, or chance. Even not making a decision is a choice, seldom taken lightly. As a professional decision maker, what tools do you use to make decisions? Yes, you use your brain and information, perhaps even computer programs to generate smart information from data. But decision making is neither a linear nor a purely rational process and an array of diverse tools and talents are called upon. These include:

- **The brain:** understanding how it processes information and biases decisions
- **Information:** the ability to recognise and source good quality information
- **Other people:** understanding how they frame and present information
- **Education:** using knowledge as the building blocks of thought
- **History and experiences:** learning from one's own and the experiences of others
- **Emotions:** understanding the influence of emotions on thinking
- **Decision process:** developing a repeatable process that allows for reflection on and improvement in one's thinking and decision making.

We've explored the development of your child's brain in some detail. Now let's look at how this tool does its job and the enormous role it plays in both helping and hindering our ability to think soundly and make good decisions.

Our bountiful brains are extremely resource intensive and can consume up to 20% of the body's glucose supply and oxygen. Fully aware of its own appetite, our processor will try to conserve energy whenever possible, using an array of energy-saving devices. Mental biases and heuristics, or shortcuts, are such devices. Not only is our brain a fuel guzzler but it's also a slower processor than we'd like it to be. When I asked audiences which they thought was a faster data processor: their conscious brain or a quad-core computer, I am still amazed that the majority picked the conscious brain as the faster of the two. Would you have picked the brain? We'd like to think that we walk around with something that can't be replicated by a machine and definitely not improved upon. But if I gave you a spreadsheet with 100 figures to be multiplied together, would you say, "Oh, don't bother with Excel, I can calculate it faster in my head." No? I didn't think so.

We may be able to perceive and process a variety of more subtle data that computers can't but when it comes to raw processing power, our brains jog along at a fraction of the speed of an old 56K modem. Remember those? The only thing that I remember about them was having to dial up to some faraway server and then wait for a tiny trickle of bandwidth to connect me to the slow motion magic of the world wide web. Our brains process information even slower, way slower.

Yet some people appear to make good judgements really

quickly, such as the paramedic who must weigh up a tremendous amount of information and make a life-or-death decision rather quickly. Same for a fighter pilot, soldier or firefighter. Or the CEO that is under pressure at a board meeting to deliver a quick decision. Each of these people have a repository of past knowledge and experiences feeding into their decision-making process at speeds much faster than our prefrontal cortex (the conscious processor of the brain) can process. Such information can be bundled under the label of intuition or as some researchers have labelled it, "somatic markers".[2] In the case of a soldier or fighter pilot, they have also honed and trained their decision making through many hours in a simulator and combat training. In much the same way, executives have a range of painful and successful experiences to call upon and hopefully, some introspection into their thinking as well. Our children are still building up this huge database of decision outcomes and so many of their challenges, like many found in the world of counterterrorism, are new and unchartered.

Somatic markers and training aren't enough to overcome the limitations of both a slow and a resource-intensive brain. For that, we add mental shortcuts (or heuristics) into the thinking process as well. A stereotype is such a shortcut. We are able to gather enough information to make a decision about whether we will trust someone, or not, through a single glance. Someone's clothes, hair, tattoos, state of cleanliness, facial expression, accent and any other markers that we are able to perceive generate a remarkably comprehensive profile in our own minds. It is a snapshot that may represent some truth or none at all. It doesn't take very long either.

---

2   The Somatic Marker Hypothesis (SMH) proposes a mechanism by which emotional processes can guide (or bias) behaviour, particularly decision making. See Damasio, Antonio R. (1994). *Descartes' Error: Emotion, Reason and the Human Brain.* New York, NY: Random House

I once spent a week trying not to stereotype. This involved not forming an opinion or a "feeling" about someone new when I met them for the first time. Do you think I could turn this heuristic off and resist judging at first glance? No, I couldn't. Despite my best efforts, I received internal intel on every new person that I met, before I'd had a chance to make a conscious judgement about them. The best I could do was override my initial flash assessment of someone with much slower rational thought later on.

The Business of Bias

Behavioural economics explores the mental processes we rely on to make everyday decisions. Supported by advances in neuroscience and neural imaging, it focuses on the mental biases and shortcuts (such as stereotyping) that we generate as we process data. Add to this research in the psychology of motivation and information framing and we are starting to create a really useful operating manual for our own thinking machine. Imagine if we'd had these insights as children? If our parents could have taught us how prejudice is formed, why we use stereotypes without even thinking about it, why we believe what "they" say or make especially risky decisions as teenagers? Imagine if they could have explained to us, at 13-years-old, how our emotions affected our thinking and decision making and even ability to crack that difficult algebra problem? Wouldn't our world have been a better place?

Anchoring Our Thoughts

There are dozens of thinking biases and shortcuts to explore but don't worry, I'll stick to the most common ones that your children will face as they build up their repository of decision outcomes. Before we start, please complete the phrases below.

Americans are _____

Politicians are _____

Chinese are _____

Immigrants are _____

Londoners are _____

Muslims are _____

Christians are _____

One rainy Saturday afternoon, a great commotion escaped our basement. I could hear guns, helicopters and bombs exploding as someone bellowed confidently, "Attack, attack, now's your chance!" I tiptoed to the door and peeped in as Lego blocks went crashing. A gorgeous Arabian-looking Lego castle complete with turrets, flags and an "underground" water supply had sprung up in the middle of the room. Its mini-figure guards with turbans and rifles were being blown away by a whirring twin prop helicopter and men in blue jumpsuits with fake American accents.

"Gosh, honey. What are you playing? Cops and robbers?" I asked my son as another bad guy fell.

"No. Can't you see? FBI and terrorists!"

"And which ones are the terrorists, sweetie?"

Why did I ask if I knew the answer already? Because I didn't want to believe that, at 6-years-old, my son was able to profile and discriminate people (or in this case Lego mini-figures) based on stereotypes. I soon learnt that his terrorists were from Afghanistan where they go to school to learn to make bombs. This was shortly after the Boston bombing (2013) and the two terrorists involved were thickly spread across the media. Sure, we spoke about it but I was very careful to try to avoid the usual stereotypes. In the world we live in, feeding him stereotypes will almost definitely do more harm than good later on in his life. In addition to the Boston bombing, we had discussed 9/11 a few times and I realised that his entire experience of terrorism hinged on two high-profile events and his age-appropriate belief that people are either good or bad. He had anchored on the few facts that he knew and extrapolated them to form a mentally satisfying explanation of the bad guys of the 21st century. But not for a minute could I blame the fact that he was only 6-years-old. In fact, the anchoring bias is a mental shortcut, or heuristic, that adults are particularly good at. It allows us to focus on only a few salient bits of information and build a narrative around those. Why do we do it? Well, because it speeds up our ability to process a lot of information. And a little extra processing speed goes a long way with our rather pedestrian processor.

Now let's get back to the words you wrote down. Did you have a word for every one of them? A one-word answer for an entire cohort of people? Most of us do. Your answers will vary depending on who you are. Do you see how many stereotypes you harbour? Every stereotype is an anchor that flashes through your mind when you encounter strangers. It's our metal database dishing up lightening quick preconceived information to feed into our decision process in the hope of speeding things up and avoiding imminent danger. It helps us form a quick conclusion (yes, a conclusion) about the stranger we are staring at on the train who fits one of these descriptions. Have you noticed how your friends who are British, Chinese or American don't necessarily fit your stereotype of their group? If only stereotyping were harmless mental trickery. Unfortunately, religious extremism, bullying, discrimination and racism all spawn from these unexamined anchors.

OK, so you are trying to avoid stereotyping people in front of your children. When the cab driver from X foreign country runs the red light ahead of you, you try not to blame it on all people from X being idiots or bad drivers. That's a great start. But only a start. Anchoring as a mental heuristic creeps into almost every situation where we have to weigh up information. What we already know about something is presented to us quickly and subconsciously and becomes our starting point, or anchor, for thinking about that information. We tend to adjust new information relative to our existing anchor.

When we first moved to Hong Kong we hired a cheerful property agent to help us find a suitable apartment. She knew our budget and that it wasn't negotiable. She also knew that our knowledge of the HK property market was anorexic to say the least. She showed us loads of apartments within our budget. They varied from mouldy to stinky, tiny and dilapidated and sometimes all of these together. This was unexpected as we had thought our housing budget was reasonable. Clearly we were wrong and asked her to show us some nicer apartments as we were running out of time. Of course every nicer apartment was out of our budget. Did we pay up? Sure. Had we been played? Oh yes. After a year we discovered that there were wonderful apartments very much within our budget that she had chosen not to show us. She skilfully created false anchors for us to judge our spending power against.

The sooner our children are able to understand the effects of anchoring, the better. And not just because setting the opening anchor in any negotiations will frame the entire discussion but rather because anchoring leads to a far more insidious, hard-to-spot-when-you're-older mental shortcut – confirmation bias.

Confirmation Bias

In March 2011, I was teaching a semester of Critical Thinking at a business school in Singapore. On the 11th of that month, a magnitude-9 earthquake off the Pacific coast of Tōhoku in Japan caused a tsunami that devastated the Fukushima Daiichi nuclear power plant. This was the largest nuclear meltdown since Chernobyl. As more information became available about the genesis of the incident and subsequent emergency operations to contain rapid nuclear fallout, my students and I were able to evaluate the mental mistakes that decision makers were making under conditions of enormous pressure and international media scrutiny. Sitting in our lecture theatre after a hot lunch and shooting mental arrows at bad decisions made by others turned out to be quite easy to do. Even deciding how their decision making could have been improved upon turned out to be easy peasy.

But critical thinking in real time is not so easy or even intuitive. So, come exam time, I turned the spotlight on my students. Their final group assignment question pack included articles with emotive photos and information about both the human tragedy and technical and regulatory failures of the nuclear disaster at Fukushima. The final question was this one about nuclear power:

Considering the recent events in Japan, would it be reasonable to suggest that nuclear energy be phased out worldwide? Support your answer.

What do you think the majority of answers from these final-year MBA students were? None of us are nuclear specialists so I wasn't looking for overly technical justification for their decision. Instead I was most interested in how they supported their conclusion. The vast majority of groups replied that yes, nuclear energy should be phased out, and they cited information related to the recent disaster almost exclusively. They chose to ignore the safety and efficiency of the majority of the world's nuclear power plants and anchored instead on the outliers that had gone wrong. They also ignored influential differences between geographic locations and government oversight that would affect safety and stability of a nuclear power plant. *Recency bias* encouraged them to give almost 100% weight to the most recent event with less or no weight afforded to decades of data on the efficacy of nuclear energy.

I repeated the case study and asked this same question of the following two postgrad and undergrad classes at the end of 2012 – a year and half later. Do you think I received the same answer with the same justifications, despite using exactly the same material? Of course not. These students firmly believed that nuclear energy was here to stay and quoted far wider sources of information than recent press.

What happened? In the aftermath of the disaster, the pain, suffering and enormous damage to life and property were spread across the news in blow-by-blow, by-the-minute updates. It would be almost superhuman to be unaffected by the emotions and human tragedy unfolding across Japan – a country loved for its food, landscapes and gentle, quirky people. To suggest that nuclear power was the way of the future at this point in time would have been emotionally challenging. Eighteen months later, I received very different conclusions for the same case study. This time answers reflected a good understanding of how human error had caused the devastation at Fukushima. It was also clear that nuclear power had swung back in favour. What a difference a few months make to decision making. It's not just my students who were caught up in this trap of vilifying nuclear power in the aftermath of the tsunami. Politicians across the world were called on to justify nuclear power capacity and investment. In Switzerland and Germany, plans to extend or expand nuclear power plants were called off, despite neither of these countries having any geographical or regulatory similarities to those affecting Japan, or Fukushima specifically.

What the first group of students had fallen prey to was a bias that they knew very well in theory – confirmation bias.[3] This sneaky mental shortcut grows like a weed from a mental anchor, which in this case, was the human disaster of the nuclear crisis. Despite already agreeing that the cause of the nuclear failure was manmade and not specifically the type of power plant

---

3   Readers familiar with decision science will also pick up a dash of recency bias here.

in question, they still made a decision that it was bad for humankind. They found plenty of evidence to confirm their belief and ignored a growing body of evidence that disagreed with them.

As their lecturer, I think I failed here. What's the point of only being able to avoid biases in academic exercises but not when the stakes are high? When it really counts? You'll see confirmation bias creep in whenever you have a particular opinion on something and attach greater importance to information that agrees with your opinion and discount information or people that disagree with you.

What can be done about it and how can we teach this to our children in a meaningful way? Let's cover a few more biases and then we'll look at how to start introducing sound thinking into growing, but impressionable, minds. In the meantime, try and think of some ways you could guard against this in your own thinking.

7.2

ADOLESCENCE AND GROUPTHINK

Can you now identify how the confirmation bias influenced the FBI's case against Mayfield?

Their initial suspicion was that Mayfield was guilty. They then proceeded to look for evidence of his guilt and had enough data to pick and choose the bits that corroborated their suspicions. Of course they also found evidence of his innocence but put less weight on these "facts". What made this error particularly powerful was that it wasn't only one or two individuals making thinking mistakes but it would seem that the entire team eventually bought into Mayfield's "guilt". This is striking but not surprising and illustrates a dynamic that our older children are particularly vulnerable to – groupthink.

Social psychologist, Irving Janis, first introduced the idea of groupthink. He used it to explain why otherwise rational people can make irrational or poor decisions when grouped together.

> Groupthink occurs when a group makes faulty decisions because group pressures lead to a

deterioration of mental efficiency, reality testing
and moral judgement.

~ Irving Janis

Sounds a bit harsh, doesn't it? Team-based decision making
is a bastion of business and a model that modern schooling
encourages. But history and evidence bear out that we risk a
change in our thinking patterns when we enter into the comfort of
a group or the shadow of a cause. Groupthink is particularly virile
during adolescence (from 13- to 19-years-old), a time during which
friendship groups become particularly important. Its influence is
so pervasive in our teenagers' thinking and decision making that it
warrants a thorough discussion.

Statistics tell the story of adolescence as a developmental
stage characterised by poor decision making and increased risk
taking. Adolescents and young adults are more likely than adults
over 25 to binge drink, smoke cigarettes, have multiple casual sex
partners, engage in violent and other criminal behaviour, and
have fatal or serious automobile accidents, the majority caused
by risky driving or driving under the influence of alcohol.[1] Much
of this behaviour has been blamed on some rather spurious
notions that are not supported by research. This includes the
widely-held belief that our teens are somehow irrational or
deficient in how they process information, resulting in them
not perceiving risks the way that adults do. Then there's the idea
that teenagers think they are invincible or invulnerable to injury
or consequences. It comes as a surprise to many parents that a
significant body of research shows that the logical reasoning

1   Steinberg, L. (2008). *A Social Neuroscience Perspective on Adolescent Risk-Taking*.
     Department of Psychology, Temple University. NIH Public Access.

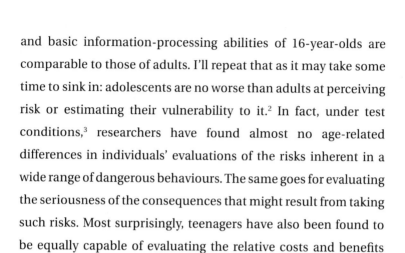

and basic information-processing abilities of 16-year-olds are comparable to those of adults. I'll repeat that as it may take some time to sink in: adolescents are no worse than adults at perceiving risk or estimating their vulnerability to it.[2] In fact, under test conditions,[3] researchers have found almost no age-related differences in individuals' evaluations of the risks inherent in a wide range of dangerous behaviours. The same goes for evaluating the seriousness of the consequences that might result from taking such risks. Most surprisingly, teenagers have also been found to be equally capable of evaluating the relative costs and benefits of these activities.[4] The conclusion then is that heightened risk taking in adolescence does not stem from ignorance, irrationality, delusions of invulnerability, or faulty calculations.[5]

Despite the evidence, the vast majority of educational interventions continue to aim to reduce risky behaviour through information and discussion about the dangers of unprotected sex, alcohol, drugs and risk taking. Unfortunately, adolescent fatalities don't reflect these educational efforts and the tax dollars spent on them. Perhaps a better understanding of the cause of these two troublemakers (poor decision making and increased risk taking) will go a long way to making adolescence a safer but still fulfilling chapter in life?

So what drives your average level-headed teenager to make questionable decisions or engage in risky behaviour such as experimenting with drugs or other socially undesirable activities and what do their peers have to do with it?

2   Millstein S.G. and Halpern-Felsher B.L. (2002, July). *Perceptions of Risk and Vulnerability.* Journal of Adolescent Health.
3   Test conditions are staged with test subjects usually knowing that the outcome of their performance in experiments will not have lasting implications for their future.
4   Beyth-Marom R., Austin L., Fischoff B., Palmgren C., Jacobs-Quadrel M. (1993). *Perceived Consequences of Risky Behaviors: Adults and Adolescents.* Developmental Psychology.
5   Reyna V.F. and Farley F. (2006). *Risk and Rationality in Adolescent Decision-making: Implications for Theory, Practice, and Public Policy.* Psychological Science in the Public Interest.

Brain imaging and other studies are continuously providing us with more sophisticated and granular explanations for behaviour that occurs during this complex and pivotal life stage.

This is what we know so far: Cognitive systems that allow for sound decision making, risk assessment and impulse control are housed in the foremost part of the brain (the prefrontal cortex). The prefrontal cortex develops linearly from birth through to early adulthood and is considered a top-down control system. However, if risk assessment and impulse control continue to develop slowly and steadily from childhood through adolescence, then teenagers should be more risk averse than younger children. If you have a teen and a preteen in your family, you may be shaking your head here. In theory, your teen should be way more sensible than their younger siblings but something interesting shifts in how your sweet little one perceives the consequences of their risk taking as they mature.

There is evidence that children are more likely to anticipate negative consequences from risky behaviour. A teen, on the other hand is more likely to associate risk taking with reward or other positive consequences.[6] This is compounded by the non-linear development of another system that reacts to reward and emotional and social stimuli known as the limbic system. This bottom-up reactionary system reaches maturity in middle adolescence (a few years before the control system does) allowing for a more exaggerated response to reward and emotion.[7] Despite the fact that adolescents can reason as well as adults, in emotionally charged or risky situations, the more "mature" reward-seeking limbic system will override that reasoning,

6   Casey B.J., Galvan A. and Hare T.A. (2005). *Changes in Cerebral Functional Organization During Cognitive Development.* Curr Opin Neurobiol. 2005a;15(2): 239–244.
7   Casey, B.J., Jones, R.M., and Hare, T.A. (2015, November 11). *The Adolescent Brain.* Annals of the New York Academy of Sciences. 1124 (2008): 111–126. PMC. Web.

creating an imbalance in how teenagers process and respond to information. This "risky" development period is shown below.[8]

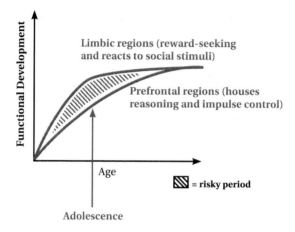

Are you starting to see why interventions that increase awareness of risks and improve decision making at a cognitive level in adolescence are often not as successful as they should be?

Hormonal changes at this time also conspire to increase sensitivity to both reward[9] and addiction, further heightening the pleasure gained from taking risks. You'll be pleased to know that the teenage top-down reasoning system begins to wrestle back control at around 15-years-old (allowing for individual differences).

It's only mildly comforting to know that these changes are not unique to humans but seen across a range of non-human primates, rodents and even bird species. In all of these species, novelty seeking, hanging out with same-aged peers and quarrelling with one's parents all appear in different forms,[10]

8   Galvan A., Hare T., Voss H., Glover G. and Casey B.J. *Risk-taking and the Adolescent Brain: Who is at Risk?*. Dev Sci. 2007;10(2):F8–F14.
9   Ibid.
10 Spear L.P. *The Adolescent Brain and Age-related Behavioral Manifestations.* Neurosci Biobehav Rev. 2000;24(4):417–463.

leaving scientists to ponder an evolutionary explanation for them. After all, adolescence is a time of transition from the security of the home and mom's cooking to that of independence, finding a mate and fending for oneself – all risky undertakings.

So until late adolescence, the drive to take risks, for the average teenager, is stronger than the ability to control impulse. Interventions to reduce teenage risk taking that focus on enhancing cognitive control systems, and therefore sound decision making, may not be addressing the real cause of the behaviour at all. Helping teenagers understand their lack of impulse control in the heat of the moment and giving them tools to cope with this might be more successful.

What about the influence of peers? If you are a parent of a teen, you'd probably know that adolescent risk taking is far more likely to occur in groups. In fact, this is a hallmark of the teenage years and the degree to which your teen's friends drink alcohol excessively or use illicit drugs is one of the strongest, if not the single strongest, predictor of their own substance use.[11] Even a supremely level-headed preteen could go on to make uncharacteristically bad decisions later on, given peer pressure.

All risks are taken in the hope of some implicit or explicit reward granted instantly or at some point in the future. Reward increases the activity of a feel-good chemical called dopamine in our brain, as do addictive drugs. The adolescent brain experiences an exponentially bigger shot of this fun stuff than the rest of us do when experiencing reward, leading researchers to believe that this is a further driver of their increased appetite for risk. But there's more: taking risks in the presence of peers (regardless of

11 Chassin L., Hussong A., Barrera M., Jr., Molina B., Trim R. and Ritter J. *Adolescent Substance Use*. Handbook of Adolescent Psychology, edited by Lerner R. and Steinberg L., Wiley, 2004.

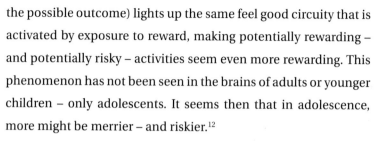

the possible outcome) lights up the same feel good circuity that is activated by exposure to reward, making potentially rewarding – and potentially risky – activities seem even more rewarding. This phenomenon has not been seen in the brains of adults or younger children – only adolescents. It seems then that in adolescence, more might be merrier – and riskier.[12]

This imbalance between a well-developed risk-seeking drive and a less-developed impulse control seems to be biologically driven and appears unlikely to be pacified through educational interventions designed to change what adolescents know and how they think. Interventions built around the idea that adolescents are inherently more likely than adults to take risks and that focus on reducing the harm associated with risk-taking behaviour are far more likely to succeed.[13]

We can't fight biology nor wish away the intensity of the teenage years so let's rather explore the mental dexterity behind our child's risk assessments and decision making and see how to further improve the quality of that thinking as we explore workarounds to biases and the essential habits of good decision makers.

12 Steinberg L. *Risk Taking in Adolescence: What Changes, and Why?* Ann N Y Acad Sci. 2004;1021:51–58
13 Steinberg, L. (2015, November 13). *A Social Neuroscience Perspective on Adolescent Risk-Taking.* Developmental Review: DR 28.1 (2008): 78–106. PMC. Web.

Author's note

I should point out again that the degree to which individuals translate sensation seeking into risky behaviour varies dramatically[14] and includes factors such as maturity level (early maturers are at greater risk), available opportunities to take risks (lack of adult supervision, availability of alcohol, drugs and car keys, etc.) and a child's general temperament towards risk taking. Shy, anxious children are less likely to take risks but could also find it hard to say, "No".

Let's also not forget that the relatively greater prevalence of group risk taking observed among adolescents may stem from the fact that adolescents simply spend more time in peer groups than adults do.[15]

Further reading

- *Risk Taking in Adolescence: What Changes, and Why?* by Steinberg, L. (2004), Published in Annals of the New York Academy of Sciences, 1021: 51–58.
- *Peer Influence on Risk Taking, Risk Preference, and Risky Decision Making in Adolescence and Adulthood: An Experimental Study* by Gardner, M., Steinberg, L., Published in Developmental Psychology, Vol 41(4), Jul 2005

---

14 Kagan J., Snidman N., Kahn V. and Towsley S. (2007, July). *The Preservation of Two Infant Temperaments Into Adolescence: Monographs of the Society for Research.* Child Development, Volume 72, Issue 2, page vii.
15 Steinberg, L. (2008 March). *A Social Neuroscience Perspective on Adolescent Risk-Taking.* Department of Psychology, Temple University. Dev Rev.

7.3

THINKING AGILITY

In 1917, Einstein discovered a glitch in his new general theory of relativity. His equations suggested that the universe could not be in a stable state but was either expanding or contracting. Except that was impossible because the universe was static and stable. He quickly developed a workaround to satisfy this fact and return order to the galaxy. At first he called it the "cosmological constant" – a constant introduced into his theory to "hold back the effects of gravity" and maintain a static universe.

In 1927, a Belgian priest and astronomer, Georges Lemaître, cornered Einstein at a conference and shared a theory that he had been working on, based partly on Einstein's own calculations. Einstein dismissed him out of hand commenting that his calculations may be correct but his physics was atrocious! Lemaître didn't give up and continued to develop his idea that the universe was indeed expanding and that the cosmological constant was superfluous. It would take another 60 years for Lemaître's theory to be recognised as the dominant theory underlying our understanding of our universe – The Big Bang Theory. Today most scientists accept that the universe originated from an incredibly dense, incredibly hot single point in time and space and has been expanding ever since then. *Expanding into what* is the next puzzle to solve. In case you were wondering, Einstein eventually warmed to this idea and later called the cosmological constant the biggest blunder of his career. Even he didn't know what he didn't know.

Awareness

Imagine a colour you've never seen before. Anything? That's tricky, isn't it? Our awareness is often limited by what we either have been exposed to or can mentally assemble based on what we already know and, particularly, have language for. If Henry Ford had asked customers what they wanted, they would have said, "A faster horse". The latter is nothing more than an Internet meme but certainly rings true today. If someone is not aware of the limitations of their mind, their biases, mental maps and predispositions, would they ever think of improving their thinking? Fortunately for all of mankind, there are enough people like you and me who are curious and open to exploring what we don't know.

Imagine if the chaps at the FBI[1] could have said to each other, "Hang on, does our verdict suffer from confirmation bias? Or groupthink? Or anchoring?" Or even, "Are we making thinking mistakes? Does our frame/prior/situation/environment prejudice our conclusions?" It would take just one person with the guts to not only question but prove to the rest of his or her team that their thinking needs rethinking.

---

1   From the FBI's case against Brandon Mayfield (see Chapter 7.1).

With your current understanding of anchoring and confirmation bias, how would you raise your children's awareness of these thinking mistakes? Offering your child the textbook definition of any of them simply won't work. This doesn't even work with adults. Trust me, I've tried it. I used to offer thorough definitions and explanations of mental biases in workshops and coaching sessions and expect my clients and students to be able to identify these thinking mistakes in their own thinking. What happened instead was that they became very good at picking out these thinking mistakes in theory and in other people's thinking. Of course, knowing when others are making thinking mistakes is a valuable skill but it's a bit like sautéing top quality ingredients in a filthy frying pan.

When you hear your children anchoring on one trait or piece of information and using only that to inform their opinion, ask them if they may be anchoring on it? Then go on to ask them if they can find information that disagrees with those anchors. Here's an example.

"Dad, Sarah gets more pocket money than I do. Her parents love her more than you love me."

This one is easy to diffuse, isn't it? What is the anchor? Correct: pocket money is viewed as the only indicator of love. And the question to ask is: are there any other ways in which we show you that we love you?

In older children it gets more tricky because we may be able to identify when they are anchoring on information but might not be able to find reasonable alternative anchors in the spur of the moment. That's OK, before they even reach puberty they already know that we don't have all the answers. Despite our lack of facts on tap, we can still offer them a framework for thinking about their world through slightly clearer lenses, encouraging them to consistently ask, "What is the anchor being used and how would the issue change if alternative anchors, or none at all, were used?" If Einstein can introduce a groundbreaking new theory anchored on current and limited knowledge of the universe, then we can all be forgiven for making the same mistake in our thinking, sometimes.

Here's an interesting example of an anchoring effect that has been found in teens. We already know that peers are a major source of influence on adolescent substance use[2] and other antisocial behaviour, at times even overriding genetic predispositions[3] to such behaviour. It's no surprise then that what a teenager merely thinks their friends are doing (whether accurate or not) significantly affects their own actions. If a young teen thinks that his friends are already sexually active, he may feel inadequate if he isn't already doing the same or justified if he already is. These thoughts become an anchor for his behaviour.

But the mind is a far more byzantine and interesting thing. What researchers have also found is that a teen's own behaviour becomes the anchor for what they think their peers are up to. To quote researchers directly, "Adolescents' reports of their friends' substance use are biased in the direction of their own use. Substance users consistently exhibit a liberal bias, assuming that their friends also use substances. In parallel fashion, non-substance users consistently assume their friends are non-users, exhibiting a significant conservative bias."[4] We call this the false consensus effect where we, often incorrectly, assume that others

2   Kobus K. *Peers and Adolescent Smoking.* Addiction. 2003;98(Suppl 1):37–55. [PubMed]

3   Guo G., Elder G.H., Cai T. and Hamilton N. *Gene–environment Interactions: Peers' Alcohol Use Moderates Genetic Contribution to Adolescent Drinking Behavior.* Social Science Research. 2009;39(1):213–224.

4   Henry D.B., Kobus K. and Schoeny M.E. (2011). *Accuracy and Bias in Adolescents' Perceptions of Friends' Substance Use.* Psychology of Addictive Behaviors: Journal of the Society of Psychologists in Addictive Behaviors.

behave the way that we do, perhaps for the same reasons that we do.

Apart from helping your teen to spot personal anchors, you can help them (and yourself) in commercial ways too. Advertising is all about using our thinking against us. Discounting the latest pair of jeans from $110 to $80 looks way more attractive than simply asking $80 for them, especially when the size of the discount, not the actual price is our anchor. Receiving a discount triggers the reward centre of the brain and when you're a teen, this is a really strong call to action. 3-For-2 special bargains are seldom real deals but again, that saving is processed as a reward and losing it by passing up the "bargain" also feeds into our natural tendency to strongly prefer avoiding losses to making gains. (This is known as loss aversion – another bias.)

It's not only advertisers that use anchoring to weigh us down; parents can use it quite successfully too. If you start out giving your teen $50 pocket money a month, chances are they'll grumble that it's not enough. Rather, start out offering only $35. This then becomes the anchor around which negotiations happen, not what their peers are getting. Any increase towards $50 is an improvement for them, a reward. The same goes for curfews, screen time, etc. Getting an allowance increased is a psychological hole-in-one for your teen, even if the game was rigged to begin with. If a weekday curfew is 10 p.m., then a weekend curfew of 11 p.m. doesn't feel particularly generous. But a 9 p.m. weekday curfew and midnight weekend curfew would sound more reasonable to teenage ears even though the hours away from the house would actually be less in a week.

Like anchoring, confirmation bias is easy to spot in someone else's thinking but trickier in your own. Think about this question: if two deeply religious people, from different faiths, were arguing the merits of their own religion, could either win the debate? A deeply religious person would, no doubt, know a great deal about their religion and harbour more facts that support her religious ideals than facts that refute them. So the more you argue with her, the deeper she is forced to dig into her collection of "facts" about her belief or details that discredit other faiths in order to support her own argument. The more you argue with her the more of an "expert" she becomes. We call this *attitude polarisation*, which is especially tricky to deal with if the person involved is also actively closed minded as often happens in religious extremism. Confirmation bias allows her to pick facts that support her argument and feel OK about it. On the other hand, a critical thinker not only listens to information that contradicts their own ideas but actually seeks it out.

This is where the parent truly becomes the teacher. Teachers in school or college work with pretty clear and dry facts on well-understood issues but you, mom or dad, get to deal with all the grey areas that have no real answers. You get to show your children not only how to think between the lines, but also give them the confidence to do so. Most of this will happen through how we *think and act on information*, not through what we teach them.

Do we allow ourselves to be openly questioned or do we see it as a sign of weakness? For example, if there is another school shooting in America, do you immediately take "sides" based on whether you own a gun or not? Or are you able to consider the issue and discuss it with your children as more than a pro-gun/ anti-gun issue? Do you support Brexit (Britain's exit from the European Union) to free your country from foreigners or have you carefully considered the financial implications? Do you dominate a discussion with your views or do you curate balanced discussions with give and take? As I wrap up this chapter, the world has just witnessed a spate of deadly terror attacks across Paris, Tunisia, Egypt, Beirut and Turkey.

"Why did they do it Mom? Why are there terrorists?" This is the question that my son and I wrestled with all weekend in the eerie glow of the BBC's coverage of the Paris tragedy. My initial reaction was to quote the news of the day, and Mr John Kerry in particular, with, "They are psychopathic monsters." That about covers it, doesn't it? They're the bad guys and there's plenty of evidence to confirm that they are suffering from a chronic mental disorder with violent (psychopathic) tendencies right there on the headline news.

I'm not a scholar of terrorism, politics or religion, but if that truly was the end of my explanation, I would be failing in my efforts to raise a child who is capable of reasoning with a curious and critical mind – a mind open to the possibility that we are not helpless in the fight against terrorism nor indeed the bully next door. So how do you explore the inexplicable with impressionable minds while avoiding a minefield of mental mistakes inherent in an emotionally charged topic? No matter how true it is, telling your children that terrorists are "psychopathic monsters" will engender even more fear and more helplessness against the "bad guys". Showing our children instead that the problem has a cause and therefore can be overcome, will do the opposite.

To avoid confirmation bias in any topic, a critical thinker will gather evidence to prove and disprove their theory before deciding. A little bit of online research reveals very clear origins of the ISIS (Islamic State) movement, their beliefs and theories. Their propaganda reveals a very clear path of action that they are duty bound to follow. Like the bully next door, the fact that they have a reason and a plan removes the mystery and fear that clouds this organisation of mass murderers. We can only change what we understand.

Author's note

Discussing terrorism with your child is an essential part of parenting today but way trickier than the S.E.X. talk. Unlike the latter, most parents will not go further than sharing their own personal view on terrorists with their children – a view shaped by their own ethnicity, political and religious beliefs and tolerance towards different ethnic groups. It's true that the facts of the matter are tricky to get to and most of us simply don't want to spend time trying to understand a criminal's motives, especially a terrorist's. In the hope of trying to ease the burden of the "terrorism talk" on those parents who want to bring more than their own views to the discussion, I researched and wrote a piece for *The Huffington Post* that you'll find at the end of this chapter.

7.4

THE SEVEN HABITS OF GOOD DECISION MAKERS

My critical thinking programmes centre around exploring and understanding our individual tendencies towards thinking mistakes. If we don't take things too personally and are willing to explore and learn about our own failings, then bias bashing can be incredibly insightful and even loads of fun. In the adults I work with, we usually discover a lifetime of bad decisions and mental mistakes that give us plenty of material to work with, but our children generally haven't had many such experiences yet. If we can't start with the past, then where do we start with our younger ones?

Regardless of age, good decision making will always begin with information. When you're a toddler, this may be inscrutable information of the emotional kind but information nevertheless. A good place to start with your child from about 6-years-old is to slowly guide them through the seven habits of good decision makers because developing good information-processing habits from an early age is as important as brushing their teeth twice daily. A little later on, from about 10-years-old, begin to explore some basic mental biases as opportunities arise.

Habit 1: Understand the Quality of Your Information

When 7-year-old Suzie rushes home to tell you that her new best friend's uncle is the Queen's (Elizabeth II) brother, help her evaluate this piece of information with a few simple questions about the source.

Q: How do you know this?

A: James, my new best friend, told me.

Q: How does James know this?

A: I don't know.

Q: Is it possible that James just wants to impress you or feel important?

A: Maybe.

Q: Does the Queen have a brother? Let's Google that.

Of course it's much quicker just to tell Suzie that James is lying because the Queen only has a sister but then she would never learn to evaluate information herself. In the long run, it's better to get her thinking about the questions to ask when confronted with such juicy news.

In just a few years, Suzie will have access to the Internet. An endless and increasingly primary font of knowledge that's easy, convenient and omnipotent. Google is the McDonalds of information – serving up super-sized helpings of data that have been processed and flavoured by those that have gathered and interpreted it for us. We all choose the quality of the information we consume in much the same way we choose between fried chicken and chips or a veg wrap for lunch on a Tuesday. If we base our thinking, and hence decisions, on quick-to-access and widely-available information (accepted without verification of its underlying data), then our decisions will disappoint on average. Quality information takes time and effort to gather, just like a healthy, well-balanced meal – there is no quick way around it.

Probing with questions to develop a healthy scepticism from the youngest possible age will expand your child's thinking and lead to healthier information choices. Encourage your middle school or older child to ask, "How do you know that?" when given information they can't personally verify. Then, get them to decide whether the source is credible and think about the motivation behind the information. Verifying information using an independent source is a valuable skill. An independent source is not Facebook, Wikipedia or a friend who "just knows that kind of thing". To find the primary source, one would need to follow the sources listed at the bottom of the Wikipedia article quoting the original researchers, for example.

If we were to run history lessons through this simple checklist, we might discover several alternative stories and views on the "facts". Of course that would take a lifetime, so let's focus on the present and future and help our children test conclusions, verify interpretations and frames and go to the source of data whenever they can. If you want to raise your children as thinkers, "Because I told you so" has to leave your lexicon forever.

Habit 2: Understand How Information is Packaged and Presented

It was Socrates who first proposed that all information occurs within points of view and frames of reference and that all reasoning proceeds from some goal or objective. In 399BC, the great man was executed for corrupting the youth of Athens through questioning that which was considered above question. Today we know and understand the fundamental truth in this reasoning and how it separates good decision makers from the rest. Without fail, every piece of information that is presented to you or your child is done so through someone else's frame. What is a frame?

Let me show you. Below is a list of numbers from one to ten. There is a sequence hidden in these numbers. Those of you who are good with numbers will have no problem finding this sequence. If you're not so good with numbers, give it a try anyway.

8 - 5 - 4 - 9 - 1 - 7 - 6 - 10 - 3 - 2

Got it yet? Most people find this sequence tricky or just plain impossible. I'll give you a clue – it is a common sequence that most of us work with every day. Does that help?

If you are ready for the answer, read on. This problem is presented numerically, which makes you think in numbers. In fact, most people only think in numbers here and calculators and smartphones are usually whipped out to do some interesting, but ultimately pointless, calculations. This is reinforced by my mentioning that those good with numbers should find it a breeze.

Very sneaky of me. In fact, these numbers are in *alphabetical* order, which is hard to see if you are in a numeric frame of mind. Of course you see it now!

How a problem is presented, or framed, can influence how we process the information as much as, or more than, the facts of the matter.

It's late summer in our new neighbourhood in London and a group of six boys play in the street every afternoon. My son has joined this little collective and discovered the added benefit of an ice-cream van that visits every weekday at around 4.45 p.m. At £2 a cone, my son spent his monthly allowance on ice-cream in the first week. Of course as soon as the money ran out, I was petitioned for more, "But Mom, this man is so kind – he comes all the way to our street just to check if we want ice cream. He says he doesn't go anywhere else in our neighbourhood, he comes here everyday just for us. We really should support him."

Needless to say, we had a little chat about this man's motives and why he would possibly come to our street on his way home for guaranteed business. At 9-years-old my son is beginning to understand that what people say and do is always framed by what they want out of a situation, consciously or unconsciously and driven by motives that are honourable or not. I can leave this lesson up to the school of life, but why risk that? In a few year's time, as a teenager, he will evaluate others' frames and motives without my guidance and use this to inform decisions with further reaching consequences.

Habit 3: Be Very Clear on What is Fact, Judgement (Assertion) and Opinion

Over a few farewell cocktails in Singapore, a friend and well-respected investor mentioned that, "Everyone is selling China". Everybody? Selling? If everybody is selling, then who is buying it? Stock markets are driven by an asymmetry of beliefs – where someone wants to sell a position and someone else wants to own that same position – so they trade. Short of a stock market crash or correction, the price they settle on will reflect, amongst other things, if there are more buyers than sellers. My friend's statement could not possibly have been a fact or a judgement based on fact but an opinion extrapolated from a trend or observation. It's fine to believe in our own opinion (self-deception is one of the oldest survival techniques and a fascinating topic of decision science) but let's be very careful when making important decisions using opinion as our raw data and not the facts that those opinions interpret or obscure.

Kids love hyperbolic opinion, too. It's not uncommon to hear things like "everyone" is picking on me or that "nobody" likes me or that "everyone" thought it was a good idea to climb the dead tree before it collapsed. It only takes a few guiding questions to get a child's (and an adult's) thinking back on track such as, "Really? Everyone? Was there not one single person who wasn't picking on you? Was Tayla picking on you? Was Lohini?" She would then have to admit that not *everyone* was part of the pack, which can usually be narrowed down to one or two kids who weren't being particularly nice or just one ring leader who thought climbing the crumbling tree was a great idea.

Habit 4: Develop a Habit of Deciding How to Decide First

Smiggle is an Australian retail chain that sells toys masquerading as useful pieces of stationery. (Their fashion-forward items have grown a large, almost cult following amongst infant and middle schoolers in Asia.) I was in our local store when a small boy and his mom walked in to clear his Spiderman wallet of pocket money. After about ten minutes, it became clear that, instead of having a fun shopping experience, this little guy of about 5-years-old, was on the verge of tears, shuffling back and forth frantically in front of a wall of bright playthings for his pencil case. His mother, frustrated with his indecision, threatened to pull him out of the store if he didn't pick something, anything, immediately. At this he burst into tears and thrust his wallet into a shelf of animal-shaped erasers, having lost all interest in that "something special" he had set out to buy. All because he didn't know how to make up his mind.

I wondered if his mom could have helped him decide how to decide instead of making it harder for him.

> Nothing is more difficult, and therefore more
> precious, than to be able to decide.
>
> ~ **Napoleon Bonaparte**

Do you know what a metadecision is? No? Chances are your child won't either.

It's the simple act of deciding how you will decide *before* you jump in and gather information, make a decision or solve a problem. It begins by checking that you are, in fact, solving the *right* problem, then asks you to decide *how* you will solve the problem – with what tools, time, information and resources and against what criteria. It sounds like a mini project plan because it is. The metadecision forms the very first step in a good decision process – it helps you to anticipates challenges, use the best tools, and gets all your team members (if any) on the same page. All this speeds up and improves the decision-making process.

Einstein is widely quoted as having said, "If I had only one hour to save the world, I would spend fifty-five minutes defining the problem and five minutes finding the solution." As much as I would have liked the great man himself to have said this, it appears to be a misquote based on a collection of articles published in 1966 that included a comment by the then head of the engineering department at Yale[1] as follows, "If I had only one hour to solve a problem, I would spend up to two-thirds of that hour in attempting to define what the problem is." I image the original is so widely misquoted because a) it's easier to misquote than to research the actual source, b) it sounds smarter when it comes from Einstein and c) because no one really bothers checking quotes out – especially when it's pasted across an iconic picture of the smiling wild-haired professor. It's also so widely quoted because every good decision maker or problem solver knows how important it is to spend more time thinking about the problem than the solution.

In one corner of the decision-making ring we have those like the little chap at Smiggle who know their options but can't decide between them, usually because they lack a framework to help

---

1   Markle, W.H., "The Manufacturing Manager's Skills" in The Manufacturing Man and His Job. Finley R.E.and Ziobro, H.R. (1966). American Management Association, Inc., New York.

them decide or criteria against which to judge their choices. In the other corner we have those that dive in to solve the problem or make a decision before thoroughly exploring their options or understanding the issue itself. These characteristics are deeply rooted in an individual's tolerance for risk and uncertainty.

You've seen both adults and children alike jump right in to solve a pressing task without first thinking about how they are going to go about solving it or even if they should solve it. When I ask groups of well-seasoned, senior executives to build a device that can safely land a raw egg on the conference room floor from a height of two metres, 90% of them assume they have to build some kind of parachute to do so – an egg shuttle.

Surprisingly, most groups simply jump in and experiment with the materials I've supplied. Planning or prototyping is usually not considered, nor is looking for ways in which this has been done before without needing a cleaning crew in the conference room. Almost no one asks if they have to use only the materials supplied and no one has ever attempted to solve a different problem such as making the landing surface soft enough to support a falling egg. The latter is a far easier problem to solve by turning a standard conference room chair upside down and making a "trampoline" with the balloons supplied (I supply a goody bag of materials) or tie a T-shirt across the four legs of the chair and voilà, your egg will be caught and supported if enough flex is allowed. In six years of conducting this experiment with participants around the world, this particular solution has never been presented despite being the first YouTube video that pops up if you google "how to drop an egg without breaking it". But that's not what surprises me most. It's rather that executives, who are by and large professional decision makers, don't have a framework for thinking about how they will make a decision or a strategy to guide them. Like our children, they simply jump in and get busy with finding a solution.

In their book, *Winning Decisions*,[2] authors Russo and Schoemaker chide amateur decision makers for spending most of their problem-solving time (75%) on gathering information and coming to conclusions at the expense of understanding frames, thinking about how they will decide and learning from experience – both their own and others'. They also note that a carefully-constructed metadecision can save time and money.

If you have children who bolt after every good idea or jump straight in to solving problems without pausing to think of the best way to do it or even if it should be done at all, it would help them tremendously to share the idea of *deciding how to decide* first in a few child-friendly steps. If your child is the opposite and can't seem to decide or get started on a project, then this is a useful structure for them, too:

Step 1: What is the actual problem that I am trying to solve or the decision I have to make?

Is it whether the egg must land on the ground without cracking or simply survive a two-metre fall? Is it to buy a toy that I can play with alone, that will last more than a few months or that my friends will think is cool?

I'm carpooling at the moment and "what I want to be when I grow up" was a topic of discussion in the car yesterday.

Friend 1 (10-years-old) said, "I want to be a particle physicist."

2   Russo, J.E. and Schoemaker, P. J.H. (2001) *Winning Decisions: Getting It Right the First Time.* New York: Bantam Doubleday Dell

Friend 2 (9-years-old) said, "I want to run an engineering business."

Of course I had to jump in with a few questions and I learnt that Friend 1 wants to be a particle physicist because science is fun and he wants to have fun when he grows up. He likes science and knows all about atoms. Friend 2 doesn't know what kind of engineer he wants to be but he knows that engineers design and build things and that's what he wants to do (possibly because he's a Lego junkie) as well as being the boss. We're a long way from wanting to be pilots and postmen but I think that Friend 1 is solving the wrong problem. The question he should be asking is what can I do that is scientific and fun? I suggested being a MythBuster. He wasn't sure if his dad would be OK with that.

Step 2: Once the crux of the issue being solved is known, then our problem solver can move on to the rest of the metadecision

- What resources do I have to solve this problem (tools, other people, information)?
- How much time can I spend working on this problem?
- How will I know when I've decided or solved the problem?
- Have I, or anyone I know, had a similar problem before and how did I/they solve that and what did I/they learn from it?

So our little chap at Smiggle is still standing there in a puddle of his hard-earned coins fending off his mom's frustration. How can she help him?

Clearly he wants to spend his money so she could begin by helping him decide if he wants something to play with or something to colour in with. Then help him count his coins and understand what items fall within his budget. What about the colour? If pink and purple are out then he's left with blue, green and orange and if green is his favourite colour then he's down to a handful of objects to choose from. Now comes the crunch. She could ask about the last toy he bought from Smiggle and how long it lasted, or how much he played with it and steer him towards more robust choices.

Putting a child under pressure to make a quick decision generally promotes poor decision making and misses a fantastic learning opportunity. These moments of frustration are pure gold and it's up to us to invest them.

Habit 5: Tell Convincing Stories to Understand Risk

Ahmed Mohamed[3] was the new kid at school in Irving, Texas. A little geeky, a little shy, he wondered how to fit in and make friends – an important issue when you're 14. At his old school he was known as the kid who made interesting stuff from old stuff, a cool kid. He tried the same tactic at his new school and built a clock from scratch. Not a pretty clock but one that he hoped to impress his teacher with. But instead of receiving her praise and a little extra credit for science, Ahmed found himself suspended from school later that day just before being arrested, cuffed and taken downtown to the police depot. I'm sure you can guess why. As it turns out, his clock wasn't a bomb, his school wasn't under threat and his teacher had it wrong. Like the Mayfield case, this says a lot about modern life and the unprecedented issues and fears

3   Teague, M. (2015, September 18). *Ahmed Mohamed is tired, excited to meet Obama – and wants his clock back.* The Guardian. Retrieved from www.theguardian.com/us-news/2015/sep/17/ahmed-mohamed-is-tired-excited-to-meet-obama-and-wants-his-clock-back

that we face as civilians. It also says a lot about the environment within which our children make decisions today.

As our right to be fearful increases, we seem to be reaching a tipping point where tolerance of fear outweighs tolerance for risk. Our children are growing up as the most protected generation with more protective legislation, rules, schools and playgrounds than ever before. Being more sheltered from risk means that they are also less exposed to the idea of risk taking. You may find that you tell your children when something is dangerous and why it's dangerous rather than let them even *think* about the inherent danger or adverse consequences by themselves. Don't worry, I'm not going to suggest that raising free-range kids is the way to go, but in order to raise *thinkers*, understanding risk and how to think and talk about it is very much a part of the process.

In the corporate environment, we like to leave all things to do with risk up to the risk manager and his or her flock of actuaries and number-hugging PhDs. Unfortunately, this behaviour is in itself risky business. If decision makers don't have a strategy beyond models and numbers, to grapple with unprecedented risks and imagine the unimaginable, then unimaginable things will continue to blindside us. The subprime crisis that swept global markets in 2007/2008 has largely been labelled a crisis of imagination, where politicians and governments alike failed to imagine that such an outcome was possible and later admitted so. I try not to use the word "imagine" with my corporate clients but no other word seems to fit the bill as snugly. Their risk processes failed to flag the risk of global systemic failure or the possibility of a bank run because the risk systems used had been programmed by minds that couldn't, or wouldn't, imagine such an extreme financial event.

> Problems with individual financial sectors were
> identified, but a global failure of imagination
> meant no one anticipated this crisis. No one
> stopped to think "what if".
>
> ~ **Michael Coogan, Director General of the**
> **Council of Mortgage Lenders**

All decisions involve risk – the more important the decision, the larger the risk, but also the reward for getting it right. Risk assessment and management tools are only as useful as the skills of those who programme and interpret them. Housing bubbles from ill-thought-out economic policy, stock market crashes, bank runs and corporate failures are part and parcel of our complex and risky political, financial and social environments. The risks that drive extreme events are usually the ones that no one paid attention to or could have foreseen when making the decision or setting policy. Whilst it's very hard to know what you don't know, the ability to imagine alternative futures is becoming more important around the boardroom table.

Despite being better educated about the risks our children face, we might not have a better strategy to help them factor risk into their decision making. One strategy that is gaining traction in boardrooms and on management training programmes around the world is also something that already comes naturally to our children: telling stories or creating narratives.

History has shown us that the most unlikely scenarios at the beginning are the ones that do the most damage at the end. In trying to understand the risks inherent in their decisions or actions, encourage your children to create narratives of future scenarios from the most likely to the most "impossible". They can even create stories with real or imagined characters to populate their scenarios.

Ahmed Mohamed is well aware of the fact that he is a Muslim living in Texas; even at 14, he's sadly already had his fair share of prejudice because of this reality. There are many different things he could have made to take to school. If he understood the metadecision process he could have begun by asking himself what problem he was trying to solve: trying to impress his teacher, trying to impress his school mates, trying to get noticed, or, more sinisterly, trying to get press coverage or possibly test the school's racial profile or tolerance? Whichever one of these he chooses will inform a very different invention. A ticking clock in a box that was not invented from scratch could easily be slotted into any one of these narratives. The most extreme ending to such a story would be what actually happened in reality, or even worse. His parents could have helped him choose an invention that would have achieved his aim without having to live through such a traumatic experience. Unless the risk was worth the payoff, whether intended or not.

Our children will face risks about whether to accept a dare or not, to befriend strangers on Facebook or other sites, to sneak out and go to parties without telling us, or more simply, to spend all their pocket money every month without ever saving a dime. Far from wanting them to be afraid of life, we want them to understand life better and the full range of options and consequences available to them.

Habit 6: Examine the Impact of Emotions on Your Thinking Before You Make a Decision

Did you know that the hormones that make you feel sad also promote thinking and that feel good hormones increase your appetite for risk in much the same way that being angry does? Emotions result from a cocktail of hormones or biological chemicals generated in response to information we receive (and interpret) through our own five senses. We can't remove the effect of emotions on our thinking but we can identify them and ensure that, when making important decisions, we control for their effects on our mental state – whether that be tiredness, frustration, disappointment, confidence after a success or irritation at our friends, teacher or boss. Every one of these impacts how we process and frame information. This is such an important aspect of raising thinkers that we'll devote a chapter to looking at how emotions affect thinking and decision making. We'll also look at how we can help our children become aware of not only their own emotional state but the influence that it has on their actions.

Habit 7: Judge Decisions, Including Your Own, by Their Process, Not Their Outcome

A fundamental premise of decision science is that good decisions are never random inspirations hastened by a moment of genius

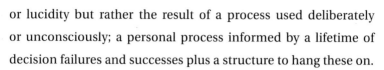

or lucidity but rather the result of a process used deliberately or unconsciously; a personal process informed by a lifetime of decision failures and successes plus a structure to hang these on.

Do you have a decision-making process that allows you to reflect on and refine your approach to problem solving? I won't dictate a decision process as it's as personal as your belief system but sound, repeatable processes usually make space for:

- A metadecision
- An understanding of how information is framed
- Checking for motives, mental mistakes and biases in all stakeholders
- Counteracting the effect of strong emotions
- Thorough scenario analysis or reality testing

If your child is still too young to embrace a process for thinking about his thinking then simply encourage him or her to STOP and THINK – if we can learn simple slogans such as "Reduce, Reuse, Recycle" or "Stranger Danger" or even "Slip, Slop, Slap on Sunscreen" in the summer, then STOP AND THINK is just as easy to remember.

7.5

SOCRATIC THINKING

A few weeks ago, I spoke at a philosophy club at a school in Surrey, UK, for students from 9-years-old and up. I planned to share a little about Socrates (he's a real crowd pleaser) and Socratic questioning. Given that this was a "premium" private school with a reputation for being non-mainstream and much more focused on knowledge than testing, I had high hopes that what I was going to share on Socratic questioning was already old news to them.

Unfortunately, I was again surprised by the students' lack of a critical thinking framework; in fact they lacked any framework for thinking about information. The idea that they could question a question was as foreign to them as poverty. Every question I posed was quickly wrapped in answers and opinions. These children were quick on the draw – knowing only that answers must follow questions. But what if a question followed a question?

Two and a half thousand years after he lived, Socrates' ideas still push us forward and are fundamental in our explorations of science, technology, law and pretty much every other field of human advancement. If you don't know it already, I'd like to introduce you to his method of enquiry, the first of its kind ever recorded (not by him but his student Plato and others) – a method that we still use today as a warm welcome to critical thinking for people of all ages. As a systematic method of enquiry, it aims to separate belief from truth, provoke deep thinking and elicit curiosity and epistemic humility. A question is answered with another question with an attitude of genuine curiosity and then another question until we understand the true nature of the problem.

Please put your hands together and welcome Socrates and his quirky system of questioning. Once you've done that, fold up the corner of this page and tag it, because you'll use it again and again – guaranteed. Please feel free to explore these questions with your child on any topic, especially those issues where the facts are often anecdotal and opinion drives belief instead – like discussions on climate change, refugees, human rights and, for the brave among us, religion, the need to fit in or stand out or even gender equality.

As always, I'll show you how it works with an example that I've already used with children. In this case, 9- and 10-year-olds. The question was: should we allow smart drugs in schools? (Cognitive enhancers that temporarily bestow lucidity, wicked processing speeds, seemingly unlimited memory storage and generally make thinking a more fun and sparkly affair.)

"Nooooooo," boomed a colourful collection of accents from the horrified expressions of the small group of boys in front of me. Clearly they've been taught that "drugs" are bad. "What if the bad guys get hold of them?"

I wasn't there to talk about the drug itself, which is by now

available legally in the form of Modafinil. I was interested in helping them work through the question and to identify the influence of their beliefs on their conclusions using Socratic questioning. This is how it went – I introduced six groups of questions that would help us debate this idea:

1. Questions for clarification:

What do you mean by...?

Could you put that another way?

What do you think is the main issue here?

So, we can ask:

- What is meant by *smart drugs* – clarify which drug you are talking about, its effects and side effects.
- What is meant by *allow* – is it allowed for everybody or only those with learning difficulties? Is it allowed by prescription or can anyone just take it? Must a student tell a teacher if they are taking it? Must they get permission first?
- Is the issue about the safety of the drug, the effects of the drug or the social effect in the classroom?

Can you see how ambiguous and open to interpretation our original question was?

2. Questions about the question:

Are we asking the right question?

Why is this question important?

Is this question easy or difficult to answer?

Why do you think that?

Does this question lead to other important issues and
questions?

Once we've clarified the question, we may want to change it to better reflect its actual meaning. Perhaps one of the following is more accurate: Are smart drugs safe to use? Do they create an unfair advantage? Should children with learning difficulties be offered smart drugs? Should just Modafinil be banned or all forms of cognitive enhancement?

Naturally this leads to all sorts of derivative issues and questions about doping and bad guys and unfair advantages. But also questions about superhuman enhancements and their implications for all of us. No matter where you stand on the issue, it's no longer the sole realm of superhero blockbusters and science fiction but rather something our children will have to deal with in their lifetime.

3. Questions that probe assumptions:

What are we assuming (guessing) but not sure of?

What could we assume instead?

How can you prove or disapprove that assumption?

Here the children definitely assumed that all drugs were bad and had bad side effects (well done, life skills class) but a little bit of research revealed that the benefits of this particular drug far outweighed the physical side effects. The military (both the good guys and the bad guys) already have it on their approved list and so do about a quarter of Oxford University's students – keep up, will you!

The rest of the questions follow a similar and natural pattern of probing ideas and gathering information to form new ones or confirm existing ones.

4. Questions that probe reasons and evidence:

Do we have enough evidence?

Is our information from reliable sources?

Are we anchoring on any one piece of evidence or idea?

Do we have information from different sources or just ones that agree with us? (confirmation bias check)

5. Questions about viewpoints and perspectives:

What is another way to look at it? (checking for framing)

What are the strengths and weaknesses of our current viewpoint?

How would we disagree with our own conclusion?

6. Questions that probe implications and consequences:

What are the consequences of our conclusion?

What are the implications of that conclusion?

Are there any next steps?

7.6

THE TERRORISM TALK

Previously published as a blog post on The Huffington Post.

Helping You Explain the Unexplainable

How can we discuss the frightening yet inscrutable concepts of terrorism with our children? As a parent, you know that your beliefs will shape your children's beliefs and actions, which will ultimately shape tomorrow's neighbourhoods and societies. Helping children understand an evil that is foreign yet right in our midst is a contemporary parenting imperative.

So how do you explain the inexplicable to impressionable minds? No matter how true it is, telling your children that terrorists are "psychopathic monsters" will engender even more fear and more helplessness against the "bad guys". Showing our children instead that the problem has a cause, and therefore a solution, will do the opposite. In critical thinking, we call this a thought experiment and, with the help of expert knowledge, it goes something like this:

Q: What if we knew what makes an ISIS fighter?

What if we knew that ISIS fighters who had been interviewed

in prison are generally ignorant about the religion and politics of their paymaster, that they know little of its most extreme requirements? What if we knew that the average age of a fighter is 27, with 2 children? That they came of age in a war-torn Iraq during the American occupation that began in 2003. As teenagers they couldn't go out to parties or even have girlfriends. Many of them grew up without fathers. They blame the Americans for this and leaving them in the middle of a civil war where food, safety and shelter were scarce and fear was plentiful, violence a way of life. For many of them, fighting for ISIS is seen as a way to avenge that. To take action and not wait for someone else to do it on their behalf.

Armed with information like this, we have a way of making the truly incomprehensible, comprehensible. As uncomfortable as it is to think and talk about, we can only change what we understand.

Q: What about the big question? What is ISIS?

What if we knew that ISIS was formed around ancient texts called the Prophetic Methodology? Texts that followers are not allowed to question, for to question them would mean certain death. These medieval texts were written at a time of war when brutality and bloodshed were the norm. Experts like Bernard Haykel tell us that the Islamic State is trying to recreate these earliest days and reproduce its norms of war. They want to create a vast empire filled with loyal subjects who abide by their extreme laws. Much like Hitler and his Nazi party, the Islamic State is committed to purifying the world by killing vast numbers of people who disagree with their beliefs. They see the world in black and white. Their propaganda tells us that they categorically reject peace and aim to bring about the apocalypse in all of its headline hyperboles, even if it means their own destruction. Perhaps this is why we find them so hard to understand, yet their propaganda is clear and available.

Q: Why do they commit acts of terror?

It would seem that terrorism is their way of making us (their enemy) feel afraid. They hope that fear will create intolerance and hatred, driving a wedge between different religions and people. Perhaps they've been watching Star Wars reruns and know that hatred is the path to the dark side. If we are weak, full of hatred and focused on what divides us more than what unites us as people, we will be easier to conquer.

Q: Am I powerless to help?

While the the leaders of the free world go to war against ISIS, hunt their leaders and stop young people from traveling to Syria to join them, what can we do? We can fight a movement that is closing young minds to the beauty and potential of a free world by opening our children's minds to their own power. This means giving them information and tools to think critically, to probe and dissect confusing information and the permission to question everything. Everything.

Because physical freedom is nothing without freedom of thought.

Sources and notes

- Lydia Wilson's report at www.thenation.com/authors/lydia-wilson/
- Graeme Wood's study of "What ISIS Really Wants" as published in *The Atlantic*, March 2015
- Bernard Haykel, the foremost secular authority on the Islamic State's ideology. Haykel is professor of Near Eastern Studies and the director of the Institute for Transregional Study of the Contemporary Middle East, North Africa and Central Asia at Princeton University.

TIPS AND TAKEAWAYS FROM CHAPTER 7

1. Each of us has an array of thinking tools at our disposal to compensate for the speed of our pedestrian processor. Thinking mistakes or mental biases are inbuilt compensators that require careful attention.

2. Talking through these biases with our children raises awareness of their thinking mistakes (and ours).

3. Your children will learn more about thinking and making good decisions from how you think than how you tell them to think.

4. Discussing the seven habits of good decision makers is a great way to introduce critical thinking to your children. The habits are: 1) Understand the quality of your information. 2) Understand how information is packaged and presented. 3) Be very clear on what is fact, judgement (assertion) and opinion. 4) Develop a habit of deciding how to decide first. 5) Tell convincing stories to understand risk. 6) Examine the impact of emotions on your thinking before you make a decision. 7) Judge decisions, including your own, by their process, not their outcome. If all else fails, simply STOP and THINK!

5. Socratic questioning is a systematic way of deconstructing information and thinking about our thinking that children will find easy and fun to do.

8.1

EMOTIONAL INTELLIGENCE IN THE HUMAN AGE

After queuing in the sweltering Singapore heat for what seemed like half my adult life, I finally found myself looking straight into the enormous, brilliant steel-blue eyes of Optimus Prime. He was so close I could touch him. Fear seeped from his vents as he asked me to help protect the Allspark from Megatron for the sake of humanity. It would be dangerous. I'd need courage, tenacity and sturdy shoes. I took a moment to consider my options.

"Ok, I'll do it!" Besides, I was buckled up inside one of the good guys already. What could go wrong?

Autobot Evac and I pounded through the dark, deserted streets of some inner city, smashing bad bots and flinging their parts aside with no concern for the city's infrastructure or residents. Every fibre of my being was jolted and jarred, exhilarated, scared witless and completely exhausted when we finally rammed the Allspark into Megatron's chest and tumbled from the 50th floor of a high-rise building. I dropped my 3D glasses. What a battle. I, I mean we, had saved the day and the earth in under five minutes. I needed a strong cup of tea after that.

My first experience with immersive virtual reality was so convincing that the only thing I found disorientating when the lights came on was the fact that I was still sitting in the same seat, in the same carriage, in the same place on the Transformers ride at Universal Studios, that I had been when this wild adventure started. I felt like I'd peered into the future of entertainment, of communication and so many other things. But no, the future was already here, five minutes into my past.

The virtual component of our reality is growing in every area of our lives – from cultivating virtual relationships to physical thrills, medical diagnoses, answering our questions in full sentences, playing games against us and even doing our bidding online with a bit of sass – thank-you Apple and Siri. What steam power did for physical labour, technology is doing for mental labour. Computing has only been around since the 1950s and like a new toy, we are still learning its rules, implications, boundaries and possibilities.

The brainchild of information technology, artificial intelligence, is taking computing to the next level by challenging conventional reality as it easily steps up to more traditionally human roles such as quality control, call centre staffing, virtual companions and disease diagnostics. Going forward, the need for skills that computers would find hardest to fulfil will most likely be more in demand than ever. Futurologists and human resource professionals caution us not to ignore the uniquely human skills of leadership, motivation, innovation and emotional intelligence as they will continue to look better and better on CVs. These skills will no longer be seen as just part of our personality but as essential to a successful career. They see a commercial world clustered into roles fulfilled by technology, roles performed by those who program and create technology and roles requiring human skills that technology would find hard to replicate, such as motivating an increasingly dispersed or disparate workforce and connecting meaningfully with employees as well as customers.

This is a sentiment echoed by Ramez Sheikh, the charismatic Vice President of Network Development and Distribution at Universal Networks Asia, part of media giant NBC Universal. He shared a breakfast with me in downtown Singapore and his refreshingly authentic views of leading and motivating a high-performing sales team that swims with the big sharks in the world of multimillion-dollar entertainment deals. "My greatest challenge," he says, "is to engage my staff in what they are doing. To help them find meaning in their role through understanding the value they bring. A leader must be able to create a narrative, an evolving story that people can relate to. To decode complexity – to take a lot of information and distil it into something individuals can understand and connect to." No piece of software can do this yet, no matter how smart it is. There will always be a role for the human element. In fact, this role is growing faster than ever as we move out of the *Information Age* and into the *Human Age*.

As this new social and corporate landscape morphs into view, we can see that preparing our children to navigate its terrain in search of fulfilment and success will require both tried and tested as well as entirely new skills. Dr Travis Bradberry is the award-winning co-author of the bestselling book, *Emotional Intelligence 2.0*, and the co-founder of TalentSmart, the world's leading provider of emotional intelligence tests and training, serving more than 75% of Fortune 500 companies.[1] Yes, that's quite a plug for Dr Bradberry but it serves as a frame to set the scene for what his team's research shows us. Their research concludes that, "intelligence only explains about 20% of how you do in life; much of the other 80% comes down to emotional intelligence (EI). EI is a skill that's so important that 90% of top performers in the workplace have high EQs (emotional quotient – the measurement of EI) and people with high EQs make $28,000 more annually than those with low EQs."

The big question now is whether we are stuck with the level of EQ we left home with as young adults or can we gain emotional smarts as we go? Dr Bradberry wouldn't have much to sell us if we were stuck with the EI of our teenage years so yes, EI *is* a learned skill based on one essential quality: self-awareness. No-one can become successful without self-awareness – unless they are supremely lucky, in which case it's unlikely that they will hold on to that success. At the moment, the race for the American presidency is in its final stages. Hillary Clinton and Donald Trump are neck-and-neck down the home stretch as the world watches, pinching itself periodically. Trump has low self-awareness and his success at the polls so far has flown in the face of leadership theory and best practice. I'll resist predicting the outcome, which will be known as *Raising Thinkers* goes to print, but should *he* rather than *she* take office, keep an eye on how effective he is as a leader when real change requires more than rhetoric and whipping the public up into a frenzy.

Emotional intelligence is the largest part of my critical

---

1   According to the folks at TalentSmart in San Diego at www.talentsmart.com

thinking training programmes. It's also the part that participants find the most interesting and useful, no matter which audience I talk to. I often wondered why this was and soon learnt that most people are not exposed to a formal system to improve their emotional and social responses until they are sent on a training programme or read a book about it as an adult. Given its importance as a life skill, this really has to change and why shouldn't that change begin with us? To help us do this, we'll explore the four main domains of EI, the brain basics behind it and how you can help your child develop these slowly and steadily as they mature. After all, childhood, especially adolescence, is the perfect training ground for emotional smarts. Let's start with a behind-the-scenes tour of the cognitive mechanics that drive emotional intelligence, because awareness must begin somewhere.

If you were to stick a theoretical chopstick through your left eye and another through your left ear, where they cross would be round about where your left amygdala sits – a curious almond-shaped brain structure. You have another amygdala on the right side of your brain. These chaps are a bit like a team within a team and generally operate by their own rules – for good evolutionary reasons. We receive information through each of our five senses. This sensory info has a choice of two paths through our brain, aptly nicknamed *the high* and *the low* road. The high road of reason shunts incoming info through our cortex before passing it through the amygdala. Remember the cortex – the thinking part of the brain? This gives us the opportunity to think about the signals we receive before reacting to them. The low road of reaction completely bypasses the cortex and shoots data straight to the amygdala. Why? Because the amygdala is where we process and respond to fear and anxiety. Its ability to hijack our thinking and direct our actions has kept us at the top of the food chain for 200,000 years or so.[2]

Now think of all the situations in which you felt that you acted without "thinking". What about when your teenager said something horrid and later apologised with, "I don't know why I said that, it just came out. I didn't mean it." Most of these situations would have been ones tinged with fear or anxiety. When your senses perceive a situation as threatening, incoming information is directed away from the thinking part of your brain towards the "emotional centre". Here a crude template of what something "may be" is provided by emotional memory and allows us to react to limited sensory information without first thinking it through thoroughly – after all, thinking takes time. Your amygdala is well connected to the rest of your brain but largely through one way, outgoing connections, making it hard to control emotions but easy for emotions to control thinking.[3]

If we can change how we perceive information, then we can change how that information is processed and categorised in our brain and hence, change the responses we are able to produce. In short, we can become more intelligent about our emotions through awareness.

---

2   You may be familiar with older theories of EI if you have previously read a book on the topic. The most popular theory is still that of the "emotional centre of the brain". In it sensory information is said to pass up the spine and through the *emotional centre* of the brain, generating an unconscious response, before heading off to the cortex where it is processed cognitively (thought about). Unfortunately, this theory has not been proven by neuroscience and falls short when one considers that visual and auditory information doesn't ever pass through the spinal cord but goes straight to the brain. It's no secret that the theory of EI is still a neurological study in progress but one researcher that is making a significant contribution is Joseph LeDoux (author of *The Emotional Brain*, published by W&N, 1999, and other books) and his team at New York University.

3   Joseph LeDoux 's lecture on *The Emotional Brain* recorded at the University of Sydney in October 2011 and available on YouTube is an infomative layman's intro to the biological underpinnings of our fear response.

Daniel Goleman wasn't the first to introduce the idea of EI[4] but he elevated it to fame through his 1995 book *Emotional Intelligence: Why It Can Matter More Than IQ*. He categorised EI into four domains: self-awareness, self-management, empathy and social skills which, he reminds us, are learned traits, not innate abilities.

Self-awareness

> One of the foundations of emotional competence – accurate self-assessment – was associated with superior performance among several hundred managers from 12 different organizations.[5]
>
> ~ **Richard Boyatzis**, *The Competent Manager: A Model for Effective Performance*

Can you put a name to an emotion as you are feeling it? Apparently only about 37% of people can.[6] If you can identify an emotion as you feel it then you'll be in a much stronger position to manage your response to that emotion and the situation causing it. You'll also be able to indicate to your overeager amygdala that being snapped at by a work colleague, or angry parent after you smashed your curfew by a few hours, is not a life-threatening situation.

With an amygdala hijack averted, the information can then travel safely along the high road of reason through your cortex. This sounds pretty straightforward in theory, doesn't it? But if the low road of response is chosen *unconsciously*, then how can we

4   Peter Salovey and John D. Mayer first used the term "Emotional Intelligence" in its current context in 1990.
5   Boyatzis R. *The Competent Manager: A Model for Effective Performance* (1982). Hoboken, NJ: John Wiley and Sons.
6   Bradberry, T. and Greaves, J. *Emotional Intelligence 2.0. (2009).* TalentSmart.

subvert our natural instinct? This is where self-awareness comes in. I usually ask coaching clients to identify a week they expect to be rather stressful for them and then keep a journal of their emotions throughout that week. In it they note every time they felt angry, frustrated, uncooperative or withdrawn, what that felt like to them and the situation that led to each emotion. This provides us with fascinating insight into their emotional language, what each emotion feels like to them and what their emotional triggers are. Most importantly, my clients see that each emotion has a consistent physical signature: anger feels different from frustration, which feels different from shame or regret. With this heightened level of self-awareness, the coaching conversation can begin in ernest.

You already know how to have coaching conversations with your children. When they recall an unpleasant encounter – perhaps they were pushed to respond rashly or they shied away when they really should have stood their ground – help them gain self-awareness with a few simple questions such as:

- How did that (conversation/situation) make you feel?
- Does (this emotion) always make you feel this way?
- How did it feel in your body?
- When you feel (this emotion) does that make you say and do things you wouldn't usually say and do?
- How does that feel?

You can do this again and again until you have worked through all the basic emotions (fear, anger, disgust, surprise, sadness, and happiness), until your child starts to know herself inside out, literally. No doubt your child will experience all of these and more throughout her formative years.

At this point I must remind you of what we discussed earlier about control imbalances in the teenage brain. Remember? An adolescent's top-down control system (overseen by the cortex) matures slower than her overeager reward and affect processing regions (partly housed in the amygdala). So our friend, the cortex, has less influence over emotions than we'd like it to have during these pivotal years resulting in increased emotional reactivity. The good news is that if you started helping your child develop emotional awareness before puberty, these skills shouldn't disappear but rather steady them during a particularly turbulent period.

To help your teen through choppy times it's worth exploring some specific effects that emotions have on their thinking – and yes, this applies to *your* thinking, too. It won't surprise you that the cocktail of hormones that leads to one feeling either extremely happy or extremely angry also reduces our ability to assess risk appropriately. We are much more likely to make a risky investment decision directly after a large success, when confidence is elevated and new risks are downplayed. On the other hand, crimes of passion or moments of bad judgement often happen in fits of anger when taking on unreasonable risk appears justified in the moment.

Your son or daughter is more likely to suffer from bad judgement when they are feeling the euphoria of winning a personal victory or are mad as hell because someone has betrayed their friendship. Sadness, on the other hand, provokes thinking. When sad or let down, we tend to withdraw from social activity to spend some quality time with our misery or seek solace with someone whose council we value.

What about the emotion of stress? Getting to know oneself under stress is an ever more important part of self-awareness. Our senses are heightened from short bursts of stress hormones as maintenance functions in our body shut down and blood gushes to the limbs, priming them for action. Short bursts of stress were all our ancestors needed to escape imminent danger. When the threat had passed, homeostasis and balance could return to their body and mind. Life in the concrete jungle is a little more complicated, though, as our natural state of balance includes the daily hum of low-level stress – stress from traffic, bills, long work hours, bad bosses, information overload or the reality of not being (thin, healthy, wealthy, good looking, etc.) enough. Our kids face exams, relationship challenges, unpredictable hormones or even problems at home. Under these conditions it doesn't take much to tip us out of our natural balance. How do you know when you are particularly stressed? Think about it right now.

I know I am stressed when:

1. _____

2. _____

3. _____

Do you believe that stress affects your health? Yes / No

Stress shortens my temper, reduces my appetite, frustrates my sleep and greatly decreases my tolerance of idiots – and there seem to be many more idiots in my life when I'm stressed. Sound familiar? But that's not the worst part. In case you forgot, let me remind you that chronic stress can lead to high blood pressure, a dampening of the immune system and increased susceptibility to common infections. It contributes to asthma, digestive disorders and cancer, and let's not forget that it ages you more quickly. Pretty scary stuff, isn't it? Fortunately, we are no longer powerless over the ravages of this insidious emotion. The new science of stress is shattering our "traditional" ideas about it and giving us new strategies in our march against it – and I'm not talking about triple wheatgrass shots here.

We've long believed that stress is the leading cause of heart disease, which is the leading cause of premature death in developed economies. A flood of new research shows us that simply believing this statement to be true raises the odds of your early demise by 43%. Huh?

People who don't believe that stress is harmful to their health have been found to experience less adverse long-term health effects from elevated levels of stress. In a large, eight-year study (see Author's note), people who experienced a lot of stress but did not view stress as harmful had the lowest risk of dying prematurely of anyone studied, including those who had relatively little stress.[7] A team of researchers at Harvard and the University of California wondered how this was even possible and explored the physical consequences of changing our minds about the effects of stress on our body. What they found was fascinating.[8]

For the average Joe on an average day, stress will ramp up his heart rate while causing his blood vessels to constrict, but

---

7   Keller A, et al. (2012). *Does the Perception That Stress Affects Health Matter? The Association with Health and Mortality.* Department of Population Health Sciences, University of Wisconsin-Madison.

8   Jamieson, J., Nock, M. and Mendes, W.B. *Mind Over Matter: Reappraising Arousal Improves Cardiovascular and Cognitive Responses to Stress.* Journal of Experimental Psychology: General 2012, Vol. 141

in this study, participants were encouraged to view their stress response as helpful and preparing them for the challenge ahead. With this new mindset, their heart rate still went up when they experienced stress, but their blood vessels stayed relaxed. The resulting cardiovascular profile looked a lot like that of someone experiencing a moment of courage or bravery in the face of adversity. This is much less damaging than the typical stress response and can explain why a lifetime of believing that stress is helpful leads to a healthier body.

It would seem that viewing stress as a sign that our body is energised and preparing us for action can counteract the physical toll it would otherwise take – a mental vaccine against stress. If your child believes that their stress response will help their performance, then we can expect them to be less anxious, more confident and importantly, less likely to succumb to stress-related ailments.

> Over a lifetime of stressful experiences, this one biological change could be the difference between a stress-induced heart attack at age 50 and living well into your 90s. This is really what the new science of stress reveals, that how you think about stress matters.
>
> ~ **Kelly McGonigal, health psychologist, lecturer and researcher at Stanford University**

Thinking differently about a situation, or reappraising it, in order to change your response is a central theme of a powerful therapeutic method called CBT (cognitive behavioural therapy).

Luckily, you don't need to be a therapist to help your child change their mind about stress. Simply, and continuously, point out that their fast-beating heart is pumping more oxygen through their system and to their brain, those sweaty palms are from their body trying to keep them cool as they heat up, the fluttering in their tummy is their stomach muscles contracting as blood is directed away from their organs (this is no time to digest lunch) and towards their muscles, again priming them for action. It's all good.

But what about your toddler? The word stress doesn't, or shouldn't, register in a child's vocabulary until well after the toddler years – years that are certainly not stress free for both child and parent. If you have a tantrum-prone toddler, hop over to the next section; if not, skip it and move on to 8.3 to explore the second domain of EI – self-management.

Author's note

A fascinating study conducted at the Department of Population Health Sciences, University of Wisconsin-Madison (see Keller, et al. on following page) showed that 33.7% of nearly 186 million American adults perceived that stress affected their health a lot or to some extent. Both higher levels of reported stress and the perception that stress affects health were independently associated with an increased likelihood of worse health and mental health outcomes. The amount of stress and the perception that stress affects health interacted such that those who reported a lot of stress and that stress impacted their health a lot had a 43% increased risk of premature death. So it's not stress itself but the *belief that stress is bad for you* that seems to manifest stress-related illness. Unfortunately we've grown up with the mantra that stress is BAD and so have a lifetime of programming to rework. It may be too late for many of us but we can still influence our children's beliefs about it.

Further reading

- Keller A., Litzelman K., Wisk L.E. et al. (2012). *Does the Perception That Stress Affects Health Matter? The Association with Health and Mortality.* Department of Population Health Sciences, University of Wisconsin-Madison, Madison.
- Jamieson, J.P., Mendes, W.B. and Matthew K. Nock. (2012). *Improving Acute Stress Responses: The Power of Reappraisal* University of Rochester, University of California and Harvard University
- Jamieson, J.P., Mendes, W.B. and Matthew K. Nock. (2012). *Mind Over Matter: Reappraising Arousal Improves Cardiovascular and Cognitive Responses to Stress.* Journal of Experimental Psychology: General 2012, Vol. 141
- Rimer, S. (2011). *The Biology of Emotion – and What it May Teach Us About Helping People to Live Longer.* Harvard School of Public Health Magazine, Winter 2011. Retrieved from www.hsph.harvard.edu/news/magazine/happiness-stress-heart-disease/

8.2

THE GIFT OF TODDLER TANTRUMS

Our toddler's stress hormones become visible to us around 18 months to 2-years-old when the dreaded tantrums begin. They're hard to miss with the biting, kicking and screaming about not being allowed a chocolate milk before dinner. The situation that provoked the tantrum can feel like the end of the world to a child but it really is the beginning of a very important phase in their life. How they learn to deal with stress hormones now sets the foundation for their ability to deal with what life throws at them later on.

Your child's tantrum results from underdeveloped cognitive control mechanisms and an overflow of stress hormones. Something (brother snatches her toy, mommy says, "no", confusion, hunger, etc.) sparks a rush of these stress hormones through her little system. Our adult body produces these same hormones but we've developed coping mechanisms to manage our response. So we avoid flinging ourselves across the boardroom table yelling at our boss that we hate her as tears flood our contorted face – we only daydream about doing it.

The part of our brain to thank is our prefrontal cortex. It helps us predict, or imagine, the consequences of our responses and use logic to figure out how to get what we want instead. But this ability only begins to develop at around 4-years-old and matures fully between 21- and 25-years-old (sooner for women than men). The toddler tantrum is not a calculated move to embarrass you or make you feel like a rotten parent. Your child is not capable of being spiteful or devious, just yet. (Telling of primary [1] lies can start at around 2-years-old[2] in the most intelligent of children but these are usually only intended to hide a transgression and are by no means premeditated.) Fortunately, the average tantrum peaks after about a minute and is usually done after three minutes, although it can feel much, much longer.

Imagine you are in a raging mood about some injustice. Perhaps someone stole the parking space that you waited 15 minutes for. Then the thief turns around and shouts at you to calm down. Does it help? Hell no, it just provokes you further, doesn't it? Now imagine feeling this way without having the ability to think through the results of your actions? Even calmly asking questions of your tantrumming toddler can enrage them further. They are not in a position to calm themselves down on cue, like you and I. Their body has to stop producing stress hormones in order for their anger to subside, which is why it seems like they don't want to be calmed down at all.

How you help your toddler deal with this natural phase of their childhood will create their first memories of stress and hence the neural pathways of how to cope with it in their developing prefrontal cortex. Every tantrum is a learning experience. Really.

---

1   A primary lie is one intended to hide transgressions but fails to take the listener's perspective into account.
2   Vitelli, R., PhD. (2013, November). *When Does Lying Begin?* Psychology Today.
    Wilson A, Smith M and Ross H. (2003). *The Nature and Effects of Young Children's Lies*. Social Development, 12: 21–45.

It provides a chance, firstly, for you to gather data on your child's tantrum triggers: time of day, level of stimulation, hunger, tiredness, etc. Secondly, for you to try various techniques to help your toddler shorten their tantrums to just a few seconds and then develop alternative coping mechanisms. Here are some ideas on how to do this.

Distract and Disarm

To stop the production of stress hormones, the source of the provocation needs to be removed. This does not mean that you give in to your child's demands – you are still the one responsible for behavioural boundaries and rewarding a tantrum usually causes more issues than the tantrum itself. No, try distracting your toddler with an interesting object that you keep for just such occasions. It can be anything really, even their favourite song played on your smart phone. Remove them from the place that sparked the tantrum, like the candy aisle or playgroup. Better still, avoid candy and toy aisles altogether.

Don't Engage on Their Terms

Sit calmly with them and let them know that you are there and ready to talk to them or give them a big hug, but only when they are calm enough. Reasoning doesn't work yet, that will start at about 5-years-old, around the time when tantrums disappear.

Tantrums tend to start with explosive anger that gives way to accompanying feelings of sadness. A sad child will reach out for comfort, usually forgetting that anything happened at all. Try shortening the anger peak with a consequence that your child understands, such as, "We can't go to the park until you stop shouting," or, "I'm counting to five. If you aren't calm by then, we are going home and there will be no iPad today." Say it once and then disengage from your child.

Tantrums in supermarkets or in the car can still seem manageable but what about that long-haul flight? When everyone else is pretending to sleep as you pace the aisle with a wailing toddler trying to escape your arms? You'll know pretty early if your child is prone to tantrums. If so, let them happen in all the *safe* places where time-out is an option. Every time the anger begins, get out your notepad and make notes. What were the triggers? What did your toddler want? What calmed him down, how long did the episode last? After three or four tantrums, you'll have useful information about what turns this behaviour on and off. Importantly, this scientific exploration of your child's seemingly illogical behaviour will also distance you from the emotions that can trigger *your* stress response system.

Gina Mireault, PhD, reminds us that, "Kids this age think magically, not logically. Events that are ordinary to us are confusing and scary to them. Confusion about the world is a great cause of anxiety to our toddlers." Anxiety can easily provoke your tiny toddler into a big tantrum.

Further reading

- Joshua Gowin, J., PhD, *Are Temper Tantrums a Fight/Flight Response?* (2012, December). Psychology Today.

- Sunderland, M. (2008). *The Science of Parenting: How Today's Brain Research Can Help You Raise Happy, Emotionally Balanced Children.* DK Adult.

8.3

MANAGE YOUR EMOTIONS OR THEY WILL MANAGE YOU

The second domain of EI is self-management. However, I no longer use this terminology when working with professionals. Self-management, or control, implies that we should routinely suppress spontaneous emotions in social settings. It was Aristotle who nailed it when he said, "Anybody can become angry – that is easy, but to be angry with the right person, to the right degree, at the right time, for the right purpose and in the right way – that is not within everybody's power and is not easy." Two thousand four hundred years later, becoming emotionally intelligent is still not easy but the returns on time and effort invested make it more than worthwhile.

Emotions such as anger, frustration or helplessness are a biological phenomenon prompting us to take remedial action. They indicate to our body and mind that we are out of balance and something must be done. Simply sweeping these signals under the carpet to remain cool and collected at all times could well drive us to a therapist's couch later in life. Apart from allowing us to let off internal steam, strong displays of emotion also signal to others that they should pay attention to us. For a small child, strong emotions are a survival skill allowing him to express a need or inner unease – especially if he doesn't yet have the words to label what he is feeling.

Chris Voss is a former lead international kidnapping negotiator for the FBI, a man trained to keep a poker face, hide all traces of emotion and separate people from the problem. Yet, his experiences in the field have taught him that emotions play a key role in successful negotiation outcomes. In writing for *Time Magazine*[1] he asks, "How can you separate people from the problem when their emotions are the problem?" He goes on to explain that emotions are one of the main things that derail communication, "Once people get upset at one another, rational thinking goes out the window. That's why, instead of denying or ignoring emotions, good negotiators identify and influence them." If we could see emotions as information, try to understand the powerful effect of these emotions on ourselves and others and allow this to guide our thinking and behaviour, then we're set for all sorts of success in life.

Before your children learn to consciously influence the emotions of others, they need to master their own. This is where your coaching conversation remains a powerful tool in their development. If we continue the conversation from the previous section on *self-awareness* and insert *anger* as the emotion identified, your coaching conversation could continue something like this:

- When you feel angry, what do you think your body is telling you?
- When you feel angry and your body is prepared to face a fight,

1 Voss, C. (2016, May 25). *5 tactics to win a negotiation, according to an FBI agent.* Time Magazine.

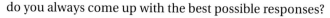

do you always come up with the best possible responses?

- Now that you've recognised what getting angry feels like, when you feel angry, can you stop and take a deep breath before you respond? This gives your brain time to catch up with the emotion and think about it a bit. All it needs is a couple of seconds.

- If you took this time to think about your response, would you be able to say something more useful that you won't regret later? Make a better argument or sound a bit smarter?

- Are there different ways that you can respond when you are angry?

Of course, it helps to talk about a particular situation and ask your child to think about how different responses would have changed the outcome of a conversation or conflict. Get them thinking about the fact that they are able to change what happens next by choosing to respond to their own emotions differently and, importantly, to put the immediate satisfaction of venting frustration on hold in order to create a better long-term outcome.

I coached a wonderful American lady once, let's call her Anna. She had been brought into a big bank in a senior position in Asia. Her husband had decided to leave his high-paying job to stay at home and look after their two young daughters. Unfortunately, he wasn't coping particularly well with this big change in his life. Anna's work hours were demanding and she seldom saw her daughters during the week. As her career flourished, her family grew increasingly unhappy in their new home and put pressure on her to request a transfer back to California, which would have ended her current career trajectory and the financial benefits it brought. She was only nine months into her new job and simply didn't know what to do. The sustained stress from both work and home had started wearing her down emotionally and she could also feel the physical effects of stress – tiredness, headaches, an inability to focus. After both her children and husband caught a stomach virus that left them in hospital overnight, she began to cry at work. When challenged in the boardroom she responded with tears; when asked to deal with a difficult colleague or project, she cried and so it went on.

Clearly this was not a useful response to challenges at work, even if it was justified by the amount of pressure she was under in a foreign country with no support and no friends. Being self-aware, she had tried all sorts of things to help her cope but remained overwhelmed by tears exactly when she didn't need them. "I just can't help it," she kept repeating to me. Our first task was to make sure that she took full ownership of her own emotional responses and understood that she was not helpless. No one can make you cry, shout, laugh or display any other emotion without your consent. You may not consciously control the hormonal (emotional) response your amygdala spits out, but you have full control of how you respond to the feeling that these hormones create within you. We discovered that breaking into tears was her body's way of saying, "I can't take on anymore." And it worked: every time she became tearful, she would be excused from the task at hand – aren't our bodies clever?

Our second task was to help her find a circuit breaker. A thought that would tell her body that crying was not necessary.

It needed to be a thought that matched the intensity of her stress response. She loved to cook and saw food as a way of showing affection to her loved ones and so decided to reshuffle her work day to ensure that she could be home to cook for her family twice a week. How did this help with her feeling of helplessness? In the moments when tears welled up in her eyes, she would change the conversation in her head and ask herself, "What am I going to cook for Emi and Angela (her children) this week?"

She didn't have to have an answer but the mere thought of doing something purposeful and pleasurable was enough to reverse her immediate stress response and hold back her tears. When tears threatened again, she'd ask herself what to put on the shopping list and every near-tear situation would add an item to the list. It wasn't long before she no longer needed this intervention.

But what if I just can't help myself? What if my stimulus-response gap is so small that my amygdala lives on high alert at the end of my well-trodden low road to reaction? Or what if it takes a lot for me to get irritated or angry but when I do, I just can't stop myself – I go for broke to win an argument? Or what if I never show any reaction at all on the surface, I bottle up my emotions as they slowly wear me and my body down? All of these seem like extreme emotional dispositions but you probably know someone who would fit each of these descriptions. Most of us do.

There's a very simple hack that works well for each of these, and for everyone else in between. I call it a *filler phrase* and it's something that allows us to respond semi-automatically in a productive way when we feel our emotions being triggered. This intervention gives our brain a few precious seconds to formulate a more useful response. They're so user friendly, our children can and should be taught to use them, too.

A filler phrase is just something that we say when we feel emotionally compromised. When our heart races, the tiny hairs at the back of our neck prickle and our faces glow red as blood brings heat to our cheeks. Everyone can choose a filler phrase that resonates with them and then use it as often as needed until it becomes part of their automatic response. Mine is, "I hear what you are saying." This allows me to slow down the conversation, without agreeing to what the other person is saying, and gives me time to stop and think before responding. I used to have a boss that would respond to every tricky question or heated discussion with a long, "Mmm" followed by, "I see" and then usually followed by, "Let me think about that." We knew he was going to say that but, importantly, he did always think about it and get back to us. Some other ideas are, "That's an interesting perspective", or, for a child, "I have to think about that", or even simply, "I don't know what to say right now."

My 9-year-old son recently came home all flustered and pink-cheeked, clearly out of sorts. Feeling his forehead for a fever, I asked him if he was OK.

"I don't know," he replied. "A girl came up to me today and told me that she liked me as MORE than just a friend!" I gave him a big hug and asked what he had said to her in response.

"I told her I would think about it!"

Oh, how I smiled – that was his filler phrase!

8.4

THEORY OF MIND

The remaining two domains of EI involve the often inscrutable emotions of other people and so things get a bit trickier. Social awareness is the natural complement to self-awareness; once we understand what emotions others elicit in us then we can transition to understanding what emotions we elicit in others. This requires empathy, a trait that develops organically later in life when we've amassed enough interactions, experiences, friends and adversaries of our own.

We know that different mental abilities peak and plateau at different ages.[1] Visual working memory peaks at around 25-years-old but working memory for numbers only peaks ten years later. Cognitive processing speed maxes out between 18- and 19-years-old then drops off pretty much straightaway. It sounds like thinking is a young person's game but before you start to feel mentally mouldy, let me share with you what benefits middle age bestows. Firstly, our ability to read the emotions of others does not peak until between 40 and 60 whilst vocabulary skills will continue to improve well into our 60s or

---

1   Hartshorne, J. and Germine, L. (2015). *When Does Cognitive Functioning Peak? The Asynchronous Rise and Fall of Different Cognitive Abilities Across the Life Span.* Harvard University & Center for Human Genetic Research, Massachusetts General Hospital

70s. Far from being cognitive has-beens, older brains continue to amass essential, non-linear skills.

So we can either wait for EI to be bestowed upon us near retirement age or, like growing a good vocabulary, we can foster it deliberately through thoughtful action. Self-awareness without empathy is akin to being a shark with an unreasonable temper that knows she's a shark with an unreasonable temper and is fine with it. If our shark ever wanted to lead others successfully, she'd have to gain social awareness through cultivating empathy. Empathy is the key to productive social skills as well as the ability to influence others.

My son has a friend who lost his mother unexpectedly. She stepped out of a train into the rain, slipped, hit her head on the pavement and passed away from the trauma. Everyone was shocked and saddened beyond words. Many of us were also surprised when the boy returned to school just one week later. Of course, the family must have been in turmoil but last minute childcare is almost impossible to get in our area. My son came home several times complaining that this little chap was annoying him and provoking him on purpose, being mean and lashing out. "He's so mean to us and no one does anything about it," he told me in frustration one afternoon.

As adults, we can understand that this boy is suffering tremendous internal turmoil and his behaviour reflects that. My son didn't join the emotional dots to make the behavioural connections because when you're 9-years-old, being sad means tears and this boy wasn't crying, he was being "mean". I asked my son to look at the school day through the eyes of his friend and tell me what he saw. He saw that his friend's mother was no longer there to make him breakfast, help him gel his hair or to drop him off in the morning – everything she used to do. "All these things probably remind him of his mother," he said to me as this very sad fact dawned on him. His friend's lunch was probably quickly put together by someone else or store bought, his mom hadn't signed his homework book nor helped him with his revision and wasn't there to pick him up at the end of the day, and never would be again. These insights, and the fact that he had come up with them himself, were truly a revelation to my little boy. From then on, instead of retaliating, my son decided to respond differently to his friend, to wait it out, to chat more to him and try to show empathy.

Trying to understand someone else's situation is not difficult but requires a bit of thought and the willingness to do so. Like an actor trying to understand the motives and drivers of a character they are to play, it involves thinking about what you already know about someone else and then guessing how they would feel in a particular situation. To help your child do this, let them play a game of pretend and ask, "If I were Shu-lin or Tayla, how would I feel about that? Why would I feel that way?"

Social Emotions in a Wireless World

With 316 million members, Badoo is the world's largest social meetup app. A 2012 survey of their members found that 39% spent more time socialising online than in person. Twenty percent of those surveyed actually prefer communicating online or via text message to face-to-face conversations. That number is growing daily. According to Nielsen, the average time spent on social media per user increased by 58% from 2011 to 2012. In 2015, social media usage,[2] averaged amongst all age groups globally, was 106 minutes a day and growing as you read this with average screen time across all devices for teens at a whopping nine hours a day[3] and six for tweens. That's more time spent consuming media than sleeping, learning, interacting with their friends in person or anything else for that matter. How much time is left for thinking, for being bored, for creating and dreaming? You may have gasped at this statistic, as I did, and then wondered, "Who are these parents who allow their children to merely skim the surface of life in an Instagram bubble of perfection?"

It would seem that it's you and I. While we are distracted by all the important stuff on *our* devices, our children are snap chatting at the bus stop, LOLing on Facebook as they do their homework and using Saturday morning lie-in time to LMAO at puppies in ponchos and other trivial bits of mind-numbing nothingness.

"The implications of this digital transformation are huge for tweens and teens, educators, policymakers and parents. For one, living and communicating via mobile devices gets in the way of empathy," said James Steyer,[4] Chief Executive Officer and founder of Common Sense Media. "Texting is so much less empathetic than having a conversation in person, looking somebody in the eye and having physical, or at least a verbal presence, with them," he said.

This new way of being in a digital world is having enormous impact on the development of children's social and emotional skills. Social emotions are the most complicated because they

2   www.statista.com
3   Wallace, K. (2015, November 4). *Teens Spend a 'Mind-boggling' 9 Hours a Day Using Media.* CNN.
4   Ibid.

require relationships with other humans – real humans.[5] Hence, exploring and understanding sympathy, embarrassment, shame, guilt, pride, jealousy, envy, gratitude, admiration, indignation, and contempt involves fostering real, messy and unpredictable relationships – relationships fostered through shared experiences and conversations.

My son's favourite girl friend (just a friend who is a girl) lives behind us so I often take them both to parties or events. This gives me a wonderful opportunity to listen in on their conversations. The most recent one was this:

She: How many books have you written?
He: I've written one. (It's true he wrote seven short chapters of his *Making of the Grand High Witch* over the December holidays as handwriting practice and his teacher had read it out in class that day, hence her question.)
She: That's nothing, I've written six. The first one is about a pony that turns into a princess. The second one happens in Egypt where all the fairies have been captured and thrown in jail. The third one is my best so far ...

She went on for the entire 30-minute car ride home. Confident and clear in her speech, she was completely oblivious that she was talking to someone who may not share her passion for ponies, princesses or the colour purple. Granted, empathy is still a work in progress at this age but I had to bite my tongue not to jump in and change the conversation while my son sat quietly listening, nodding and uh-humming every now and again. Was he really

---

5   This may change but, for now, I like to think that social emotions involve fellow human beings in a non-virtual social setting.

interested in fairies, I wondered? I asked him later why he hadn't stopped her from going on and on about the six books I'm pretty sure she hadn't written. His response was precious, "Because you said that people will like me more if I'm interested in them."

We can be so focused on teaching our children to talk that we forget that conversation is about much more than saying what you want to say or simply filling the air with words. Millennials are more confident and more vocal than any other generation. They make themselves heard and certainly have no problem in putting themselves out there as they interact with social media. You know what it's like to talk to someone who hogs airtime in a conversation with nothing but their own views or accomplishments. Now, it could be that such a person is simply self-centred or, like so many children today, they were not exposed to the social subtleties of conversing meaningfully from a young age.

I'm embarrassed to say that I only learnt the art of conversation when I became interested in the science of influence. And my wise little pumpkin was quite right because the principles of influence teach us that people are more sympathetic towards you and your cause if you ask them questions and listen to what they have to say before you jump in with your ideas. Of course, my son was eight going nine then and still trying to figure out when he should jump in and perhaps steer away from fairies to topics of mutual interest.

Now you may be thinking, "This is rubbish, I don't want my daughter to be a wallflower who can't express herself!" Remember, in order to express yourself you need an audience and a peer group to listen to your views. The ability to foster relationships ultimately rests on the ability to have give-and-take conversations. Ask, listen, speak. I'm working on the speak bit with my son at the moment.

From when your child can converse in simple sentences, start having real conversations with them. Short conversations where you are able to maintain eye contact throughout. Little ones are surprisingly good at holding your gaze. Older children actually find that harder to do as they grow more distracted. Start off with two-way conversations that you lead initially, such as:

Parent: Did you see that kitty cat cross the street?
Child: Yes.
Parent: Now where have I seen a cat like that before?
Child: Granny's kitty, Old Smokey.
Parent: And what do you think our dog, Snuggles, would do if we had a kitty like that?
Child: He'd chase it round and round and round.
Parent: I think he might eat it.
Child: OH! NO! He would never do that. I won't let him.

As your toddler gets older, encourage them to start leading your conversations and definitely waiting for their turn to talk but make sure that you do the same. Not everyone turns out to be a good conversationalist, and not everybody cares about it either, but the ability to focus, listen and think about what you are saying is a very important concept in both problem solving and emotional intelligence.

Conversations with our children are the starting point for

the development of their theory of mind.[6] This is the capacity that we have to construct a map of other people's intentions and feelings. Theory of mind develops substantially between 2- and 5-years-old at the same time as language flourishes. It has been found that children who participate in family discussions have an increased ability to predict, or imagine, the intentions and feelings of others.[7] Talking with adults exposes children to the language of behaviour and beliefs and ultimately the ability to distinguish what someone believes or thinks versus the facts of the matter.

If Johnny says to Ulvi, "I think that the world is flat." Ulvi can interpret this as either "the world is flat" or that "Johnny believes the world is flat but it may not be." Understanding that the statements – "Johnny believes the world is flat" and "the world is not flat" – are both true is an enormous leap for a young child to make and one that can only come from engaging in social interactions. In these interactions, children learn to distinguish between information and beliefs about information, which leads to an understanding of how beliefs drive intentions.

A classic example is the Sally-Anne test. Sally and Anne are together in a room. Sally has a basket and Anne has a box. Sally also has a marble that she places in her basket and then covers it with a tea towel. She leaves the room and Anne nicks the marble from the basket and places it in her box. A young child watching this will know that the marble is now in the box. Sally returns to the room to retrieve her marble. Observers are asked where they think Sally will look for the marble – those who do not yet

---

6   Theory of mind (often abbreviated ToM) is the ability to attribute mental states – beliefs, intents, desires, pretending, knowledge, etc. – to oneself and others and to understand that others have beliefs, desires, intentions, and perspectives that are different from one's own. – Wikipedia

7   Ruffman T., Slade L. and Crowe E.(2002). *The Relation Between Children's and Mothers' Mental State Language and Theory of Mind Understanding.* Child Development, Vol. 73.

understand intentions will answer "in the box" merely because they know the marble is there but those with a greater theory of mind are able to understand that Sally does not know what they know and will still look for the marble in her basket.

Apart from conversations where we expose our children to the nuances of human drivers and intentions, what else can we do to grow their theory of mind and hence social skill?

Who doesn't love a good, old-fashioned murder mystery story, one that gets us guessing at the killer's identity, questioning character's motives, probing intentions and cooking up clues where there aren't any? Unbeknown to us, scrutinising tales of twisted logic and fated relationships is also a lesson in social and emotional intelligence. The brain networks used in trying to decode stories overlap with those used to navigate interactions with other people, particularly interactions where we try to understand the thoughts and feelings of others. Stories offer a unique opportunity to explore the nuances of social skill as we identify with characters' needs, wants and frustrations, guess at their hidden motives and evaluate their encounters with friends and enemies. Studies[8] show that those who frequently read fiction are better able to understand others – this remained true when controlling for the possibility that people with higher social skills might prefer reading novels. They found exactly the same result in preschool children – the more stories that were read to them, the greater their theory of mind and hence, ability to empathise. Yes, watching movies works just as well but before you think that sitting your children down in front of the TV will have the same effect, I'll have to tell you that this increase in theory of mind was not found

8   Mar, R. (2011). *The Neural Bases of Social Cognition and Story Comprehension*. Department of Psychology, York University, Canada.

to result from watching TV for one very important reason: parents tend to go to the movies with their children and so can discuss the plot and characters afterwards but children usually watch TV without an adult or any discussion of it afterwards.

This is something I love about being a parent – knowing that every interaction with my child is teaching him something even when we're having fun and I'm not trying to teach him anything at all.

End notes and further reading

- For more on fear processing and the neuroscience of emotional intelligence, read up on the work of Joseph LeDoux who is the Henry and Lucy Moses Professor of Science at New York University and director of the Emotional Brain Institute in New York.

- Ernest H. O'Boyle Jr et al. (2010). *The Relation Between Emotional Intelligence and Job Performance: A Meta-Analysis.* Journal of Organisational Behaviour.

- *The Business Case for Emotional Intelligence,* prepared for the Consortium for Research on Emotional Intelligence in Organisations (www.eiconsortium.org) by Cherniss, C. PhD, is an interesting compilation of the value that high EI individuals bring to organisations and the value that EI returns to these individuals.

TIPS AND TAKEAWAYS FROM CHAPTER 8

1. Uniquely human skills that computers would find hardest to fulfil will be more in demand in the future than ever – skills such as leadership, motivation, innovation and emotional intelligence are already viewed as essential to a successful career.

2. Every toddler tantrum is a learning experience for you and your child. It helps you understand their emotional triggers and gather data that can be used to shorten their temper cycle.

3. The new way of being in a digital world is having enormous impact on the development of children's social and emotional skills. Help your children develop greater theory of mind, and hence empathy, through engaging them in conversations about behaviour and motivations, read fiction together and discuss the characters and how they navigate social situations, or watch a movie together and chat about it afterwards.

9.1

CAN INNOVATION BE TAUGHT?

The future belongs to those that can do two things: lead and solve interesting problems.

The challenge is that the organised educational system is about compliance, accreditation and most of all, certifying that students know how to obey.

~ **Seth Godin,** *Entrepreneur,*
November 2014 [1]

In anticipation of moving my family from Singapore to London, I made several trips to the City and surrounding countryside to explore the range of schools on offer and find one that was a good fit for my soft-spoken, bookish, academically-average son. I had a standard list of questions for the admissions person and the same list for the headmaster or headmistress. Generally, I received standard answers in return. My favourite question was, "How do you teach innovation?"

1   Dan Schawbel interviewing Seth Godin for Entrepreneur magazine (2014, November 3). *The Future of Education and the Current State of Marketing,*

My favourite answer came from the headmaster of an outstanding prep school (3- to 13-years-old) nestled in the equally outstanding greenery of Kent. "That's a great question," he replied gesticulating enthusiastically, "but it'll be much better to show you the answer than tell you." Well, this was exciting and so far the most promising answer I'd had from some 15 schools already. We donned our jackets against the October chill and dashed across a frosty courtyard straight to the art room. "Look," he pronounced, after the kids had all sung good morning to him the way good prep pupils do, "they are making Salvador Dalí-inspired instruments." He beamed. Here's a paper mâché drum that doesn't look like a drum at all. Aren't they clever?" Indeed, it didn't look like a drum, nor could a sound be wrought from it, but it was suitably Daliesque.

"Wonderful! But how do you teach them to innovate?" I persisted, "to make new and useful things?" We'd come this far in the cold and I wanted answers.

"Well, you've just seen the art class and we have music and drama – our drama department is famous for its jazzy nativity plays. That's very new. Our teachers are very creative, too."

"I see. You teach art, music and drama but not innovation?" I was pushing him; he was very proud of his master's degree in education (from Oxford) and I wanted to know how much he thought about his school's role in promoting relevant life skills.

Unfortunately, the conversation ended shortly thereafter. His parting words were, "Innovation is a by-product of all these other things and honestly, no one can expect children to innovate at this age. If they seem particularly gifted in the arts they may choose to move on to a design college from here. Although our children generally move on to the more competitive grammar school[2] sector."

Despite visiting several more "good" and "outstanding" schools in different areas, I never received a better answer. It seems the general view is that innovation is the offspring of creative talent alone. Perhaps I visited the wrong schools? Perhaps I should have visited a technical college focusing on art and design? Maybe you agree with him, maybe you think I'm being a bit harsh? Aren't creative subjects enough?

Innovation Nation[3] 2008 is a white paper setting out the blueprint for the UK becoming the most innovative country in the world.

The *most innovative* country in the *world*!

Innovation, it claims, is essential to the UK's economic prosperity and quality of life. As such, innovative solutions are to be fostered in government, business and public services. It goes on to remind us that without innovation, public services will be unable to meet their own challenges. It suggests that education must adopt innovation at all levels, ensuring that efficient and imaginative models of innovation already developed in the private sector are recruited to the best possible purposes.

I accept that change happens slowly but that paper was published many years ago and my son only has eight years left at school. His current school just bought four 3D printers for every year group. They believe that exposure to new technologies is the foundation of innovation. The kids are having a blast printing puppies and Eiffel towers – but has my son ever come home with

2   A grammar school is an academically selective state school in England.
3   Department of Innovation, Universities and Skills, UK

something new? With a new way of using a fork or a textbook? Has he been tasked with solving a new problem in a new way? Does he have a formula for doing this? No, no and no. Technology is an enabler of innovation but the spark that gives birth to a new idea has to come from somewhere.

We don't need to remind Tesla, Marks and Spencer, Walmart, McKinsey, Mercers, Maersk, etc., that they have to continuously create. Their quest is no longer merely to solve problems through innovation but to create useful products or solutions and then drive revenue through also creating the need for those solutions.

Companies that innovate are not only stocked with artists and industrial designers but talented individuals from different sectors and backgrounds who have learnt *how* to innovate. Innovation is a skill acquired in the same way as driving a car or operating an accounting package. The real question is: do schools know how to teach innovation?

The white paper's suggestion that the public sector adopt corporate models of innovation is a reasonable starting point. It sounds pretty straightforward, go out and find a working model that generates innovation, tweak it for your audience, say, a class of 12-year-olds. Teach it, let them experiment, teach them how to fail properly, let them experiment some more and then grade those 12-year-olds on what they were able to create in exactly the same way as you would grade a creative writing essay or teach honesty, responsibility and respect. Is this possible and if so, can it really be this simple?

You may be shaking your head right now and saying,

"Tremaine, you're missing the point, I'm not creative, my partner is not creative so it's no surprise that my child is not creative. I think I'll just skip this section on creativity."

Not so fast.

I don't know your child, but if you happen to believe that he or she isn't all that creative and shouldn't be expected to innovate, then I'm quite happy to tell you that you are wrong with a 98% probability. In fact, I'm willing to go so far as to say that *you*, mom or dad, teacher or caregiver, were born a creative genius. So was I – with a 98% probability.

That's a big statement that I'm happy to make. In the 1960s, Dr George Land was commissioned to devise a test to help the folks at NASA sort the most creative engineers and scientists from the rest.[4] NASA were terrifically pleased with the results and what they were able to learn from them. According to Dr Land, the test was so simple even children could take it. So they did. He used the same questionnaire to test the level of innate creativity of a sample of 1,600 children aged three to five, representative of the American population at the time. What makes this exercise more valuable than most others is that those same children were re-tested at 10-years-old, and again at 15. The results were provocative and still reverberate rather eerily today.

The percentage of children considered to have the highest level of creativity (creative genius) per age tested were as follows:
- Amongst 5-year-olds: 98%
- Amongst 10-year-olds: 30%
- Amongst 15-year-olds: 12%
- Same test given to 280,000 adults: 2%

4   Land, G. and Jarman, B. (1993). *Breaking Point and Beyond*. HarperBusiness.

Remember, exactly the same test was applied at every age group.

Land's conclusion was, and still is today, that, "non-creative behaviour is learned". I must say, his results are both compelling and intuitive. If non-creative behaviour can be learned, then surely it can be overwritten?

You know your child will have to conform at school, will have to colour within the lines and use only the methods taught to solve maths and science problems, even if they have a better method of their own. How can you ensure that they have a skills inventory to call upon when needed to solve life's unimagined or currently unimaginable problems in new and useful ways? How can you foster, rather than chip away, at their inbuilt creative mojo?

Counterintuitively, the very first step is not to teach them how to tap their creative juices but rather to build up the skill that they will need most when creating something new – resilience. Resilience is nothing more than the skill of failing successfully, repeatedly.

9.2

HOW TO FAIL WELL

> In some cultures, struggle is a sign that I'm
> learning, in others struggle is a sign that
> I'm stupid.[1]
>
> ~ **Dr James W. Stigler, UCLA**

Did anyone ever teach you how to fail? Really fail? To find the inscrutable seeds of success planted deep within the rubble of a devastating defeat?

We diligently teach our children what it takes to succeed but do we also teach them what it takes to fail? Or do we just wing it? Overcoming failure is a survival tactic and even if you don't specifically teach it to your children they will learn "failure" from you in the same way they pick up your accent and beliefs about the world.

I grew up on a farm in Africa. A childhood of fruit orchards, pine forests and endless rolling hills where my brother and I could ride our horses unsupervised until hunger or darkness forced us to return home. At 14-years-old I graduated from riding ponies

---

1   Stigler, J.W. (2014, May 19). *Struggle in the Age of MOOCs – Implications of Learning Research for the Design of Online Education.* Filmed at the ASU+GSV Education Innovation Summit.

to horses and Mona Lisa, a fiery warmblood mare, arrived in our stables. She was mine and gorgeous: muscles like twisted rope lined her flank below a chestnut coat, shiny as a new penny.

Unfortunately, our relationship was fraught from the beginning. I preferred working inside an arena while she preferred working outside of it. We were equally headstrong but Mona had the weight advantage. She bolted me off almost every time I rode her in an enclosed arena. And what does a rider do when she falls off her horse? She gets back on, again and again and again. Every rider knows this. After several consecutive falls, I grew anxious around my horse. Finally, she tossed me over her head into the crossbars of a jumping fence and shattered my nose and my nerves. Even then, the only strategy I had for dealing with this failure was to get back on. Except I no longer wanted to get back on. So I didn't. Mona was sold and I never owned another horse.

Now that's a story you won't find on my Facebook feed. There's no happy ending, no triumph in the face of adversity, no lesson to inspire others. Through this my parents taught me the only thing they knew about dealing with failure: to stand up, dust myself off and get back on the horse. Ironically, if they had taught me how to fail well, I wouldn't have felt like such a failure. If I had known how to *fall* well – falling off wouldn't have been the end of my riding career, just a phase and a challenge.

On the journey to an unknowable future, your children will fall and fail in new and interesting ways. Their attempts at creativity will be judged and their innovations will be rejected before they are accepted. Strangely enough, it's the most gifted, the most well-resourced children who seem most likely to fail at failure.

Dominic Randolph, head of Riverdale Country School, one of New York City's most prestigious private schools, tells it as it is[2] when he says, "People who have an easy time of things, who get 800s on their SATs, I worry that those people get feedback that everything they're doing is great. And I think as a result, we are actually setting them up for long-term failure. When that person suddenly has to face up to a difficult moment, then I think they're screwed, to be honest. I don't think they've grown the capability to be able to handle that."

Failing Well Starts With You

What does failure mean to you? Is it something you avoid and prefer not to dwell on? Something you blame other people for? Something you don't speak about because it's too painful or embarrassing? Something that you can almost always find an excuse for? Do your children ever see you explore your own failures or do they only see the damage and hurt left behind?

Fill these in for a quick tour of your relationship with failure:

My most public failure was:

_____

My most devastating failure was:

_____

The failure I'm most grateful for was:

_____

The failure that was most important to my success was:

_____

---

2   Tough, P. (2011, September 14). What if the secret to success is failure? *New York Times* magazine.

I'm guessing you didn't actually write anything down this time. Few people do in this section because we are talking about failure and that's uncomfortable to even think about. Putting it in writing makes it seem so concrete. If I'd asked you about your successes, you'd most likely be all over the page with your pen. Either way, if you had ready answers for any of these, it shows that you *have* given your failures some thought and not just brushed them under the carpet of things you have no control over. I'm not going to ask you what you learnt from these failures because we all take what we need from our own disappointments, if not we'd fail in the same way over and again. Without a doubt, failure has been important to you, yet as parents we go to extraordinary lengths to protect our children from it.

"Parents see failure as a source of pain for their child instead of an opportunity for him or her to say, *I can deal with this. I'm strong*," says Madeline Levine, PhD and author of *The Price of Privilege: How Parental Pressure and Material Advantage Are Creating a Generation of Disconnected and Unhappy Kids.*[3]

Professor Johannes Haushofer teaches psychology and public affairs at Princeton and found that his students felt failure, when it happened, was uniquely personal to each of them. Let's face it: anyone can look at your CV on LinkedIn and see your successes, ditto with Facebook but these only show a portion of your life's experiences and, almost never, your failures, frustrations or setbacks. To someone who is young and new at the failure game, it may well seem like everyone else is more successful than they are. To console a friend who had suffered a non-success, Haushofer created a CV of his failures. It includes every one of his research

---

3   Levine, M. (2008). *The Price of Privilege: How Parental Pressure and Material Advantage Are Creating a Generation of Disconnected and Unhappy Kids.* Harper Perennial.

papers that had been rejected, every degree programme he didn't get into and all the research funding that he had been denied. This alternative CV was so popular, and inspiring, that he published it online for all to see in early 2016, noting a meta-failure at the end, "This darn CV of Failures has received way more attention than my entire body of academic work."[4]

Both parenting lore and common sense require us to have the birds and the bees talk with our children before puberty. What if it also required the *failure* talk? For some parents, this would be even harder than the S.E.X talk but not quite as hard as the terrorism talk. It helps if we think about failure as a school subject with a Capital F and a lesson plan that can be adapted for different ages and maturity levels. Here are some ideas for a lesson in failure.

Subject: Failure

Objective of lesson: to impart strategies to fail well

Related topics that draw on this subject: innovation, achievement, self esteem, life

Timing of lesson: lesson can be administered at any time or when child is experiencing a failure as evidenced through frustration, tears, strong language and mood swings or withdrawing from friends, being unusually quiet and/or experiencing low self esteem.

Lesson plan:

1. Ask the child, "What is failure? Can you give some examples?"
2. Listen to their explanation and examples, then gently guide them with, "Failure is information."

---

4   Swanson, A. (2016, April 28). *Why it feels so good to read about this Princeton professor's failures.* The Washington Post.

Then explain:

Failure is an incredibly rich data point and important input into being successful. If success were a cake, failure would be a key ingredient. We don't always think of failure as an important ingredient in something good because it's not sweet like icing sugar or fun like cracking eggs; it's more like the bitter baking powder that interacts with the other ingredients to make the cake rise. Even if you had enough sugar, flour and egg, without a teaspoon of baking powder, you'd have a sweet, lumpy rock that would go straight into the bin.

Your failure assignment:

If failure were a school project, parents and children alike would want to know how to ace it. This is harder than you may think. How you respond to your child's early failures greatly influences their reserves of resilience and ability to fail well. How would your parenting skills in this area be graded?

If you're not sure, try this. Score yourself as objectively as possible on the following, starting with 0 points:

- When your child experiences personal failure, do you remove the cause of the failure in order to protect him from its repercussions? *Less 2 points.*
- Do you attempt to turn the failure into a quick-fix success so that your child can return to being happy? *Less 2 points.*
- Do you insist that your child find the cause of their failure and guide her in how to do so? *Plus 5 points.*
- When your child takes too long to find the cause of the

failure, do you step in and point it out because the cause is obvious and you are running out of time or patience or really just want your child to be happy again as soon as possible? *Less 5 points.*

- Once the cause of the failure has been identified, can your child explain, in her own words, how the fault caused the failure? *Plus 5 points.*

- Do you tell your child how to fix the fault that caused the failure so that he can get on with it and be happy again? *Less 5 points.*

- Do you teach your child how to blame others for the fault that caused the failure by pointing out others' failures? This might include terms such as, "It's not your fault that nobody bought your lemonade, this neighbourhood is full of selfish people." *Less 10 points.*

- Do you help your child plot the steps that led to their failure and then look for the leverage point, or points, that could have changed the outcome – as illustrated in the case study below? *Plus 10 points.*

If you scored positively, then congratulate yourself. Most of us don't get more than an F for teaching our children how to fail well.

Case study: Lonely Lemonade Stand

Jimmy wants to buy 10 packs of *Match Atax* playing cards – the latest football card game craze. He has no cash because he spent his pocket and birthday money on a Lego Star Wars Death Star kit. However, a prodigious lemon tree grows in his back garden and

1kg of sugar sits on the pantry shelf. Lemon and sugar is mixed with fizzy water from his SodaStream machine and offered to the children in the nearby playground on Friday afternoon at 4 p.m. Jimmy is a shrewd business boy and knows that if he hands out too many samples, less children will actually buy the drink. He gives samples to his two best friends only. They drink it, don't say much and move on to the swings. One mom feels sorry for Jim and buys a cup but doesn't drink it. No one else buys any lemonade. Jimmy is devastated and goes home with big tears and a heavy heart. He tells his dad how awful it was out there in the sun and how he thought he did everything right but it still didn't work. He also reminds his dad that, instead of asking for extra pocket money, he used his own initiative and tried to help himself but now is left with no cash to show for his efforts and flat lemonade that can't be reused.

If you were Jimmy's parent, what would you do next? I would be incredibly proud of my Jim boy. I'd most likely top up his piggy bank to reward his independence and efforts – clearly he deserves those *Match Atax* cards. I might subtract the cost of the bag of sugar though, because Jimmy should understand input costs.

This would leave Jimmy with nothing to help him deal with bigger failures later on. Failure may be data of the richest kind, but unless you extract it from a situation, it remains worthless. What is this data telling us and how can we help Jimmy make the most of it? The answer is not, "I'll ask Jimmy what he learnt from this", because without your guidance Jimmy may only learn that he can't rely on his friends to support him.

Getting an A for Failure

Try this rather:

Help Jimmy understand what variables were involved in the failure – time of day, day of week, lemonade, location of stall, taste testers, price charged, parents' cash on hand, etc. Ask Jimmy to think about each one in relation to his ultimate goal which was to get children in the playground to buy (not necessarily drink) a cup of his lemonade.

Let's have a look at some of those variables:

Time of day: Kids come home on the school bus at around 3:30 p.m. They usually have a snack and then they hit the park armed with water bottles full of cold water because it is hot, hot, hot in Singapore.

Location of stall: In the playground and very visible.

Taste testers: These were his friends and even if the drink was awful, they wouldn't tell him because they wouldn't want to hurt his feelings.

Cash: Kids don't carry cash. They didn't know that Jimmy would have a pop-up stall on a random Friday afternoon. He didn't advertise. Nannies and parents usually don't bring handbags down to the neighbourhood park and don't really want to drag the kids back home to get 50c for a glass of lukewarm lemonade.

Can you see how Jimmy could work through each of these data points by himself and think about what he could change in order for his stall to make money? Jimmy's dad could simply pay away his pain with extra pocket money or help him create a diagnostic template for Project Failure.

Children who are encouraged to diagnose and understand their small "starter" failures will be better equipped to deal with the bigger ones that will inevitably come later in life – as we've already discussed in the chapter on coaching kids to make better decisions. They don't necessarily need to correct their past failures; maybe Jimmy decides that beverages aren't his thing and chooses to wash the car for extra cash instead.

Fear of Failure

If failure is a rich source of data, fear is a virtual virus that corrupts our ability to read this data properly. Our lesson plan on failure isn't complete until we look at the crippling effect of fear on our children's ability to fail well and grow from the experience. Fear is an automatic reaction to the perception of present or future danger that allows our body to generate either a suitable, or a learned, response to such stimuli. Humans and animals can learn to fear just about anything – real or imagined – if conditioned appropriately. The fear response is stronger than most other instinctual survival skills. Lab rats given an electric shock after food will eventually stop eating entirely and starve to death. Granted, a lab rat may not fully understand the consequence of malnutrition and I'll sidestep the ethics of this, too, but they'll go so far as to short circuit survival instincts to allay a fear.

My son has a wild imagination. I don't. Many times I find myself saying to him that what happens in his stories and theories is not probable or even possible. So when he invents some new crazy theoretical contraption that will turn Saturn's rings into sources of energy for Earth, I'm quick to point out that Saturn is too far away, we don't know what its rings are made of and besides, do we really want to go and exploit yet another planet, etc. Bad mommy, I know, but I live and breath critical thinking all day, and risk and scenario analysis are in my blood. Over time, he will change his theories to ones that *I* approve of, more practical ideas using known elements that I can grasp because he wants me to engage with him and his ideas. His thinking will become more realistic, less inventive and less creative. Am I really helping him on his path by forcing him to explore only what is known, practical and possible? Only what *I* can understand with my very limited understanding of the world?

Look at these common barriers to creativity:

Fear of judgement
Fear of rejection
Fear of change
Fear of making a mistake
Fear of failure
Fear of the unknown
Fear of looking foolish
Fear of being different

Now tell me how many of these are we born with and how many do we acquire through experience? Correct: the only fears we are born with are those that will keep us alive – fear of danger, hunger and isolation. Everything else is learned and as our children's first and most influential teachers, we teach them to fear most of these, usually with the noblest intentions. Protecting our children from all manner of life's nasties is easily achieved through an elevated level of fear. For example, if we teach them to fear all dogs, they will never be bitten, if they fear all strangers, it will be hard to kidnap them and so on. I know a single mother who taught her son to fear the ocean. So crippling was his fear that, on a holiday at the seaside, he refused to swim with the other boys in the surf. I later found out that his mother had never learnt to swim.

Fear of failure in the classroom can be inhibiting. For many children, the more they struggle to get the right answer, the more they fear not only failure but looking foolish and being judged. Especially in Western cultures, "where from very early ages struggle is seen as an indicator that you're not very smart," says Jim Stigler, Professor of Psychology at UCLA.[5] He continues, "it's a sign of low ability – people who are smart, don't struggle, they just naturally get it, that's our folk theory." Stigler compares a typical Western approach to failure and struggle with the Confucian heritage approach where struggle is an essential part of the learning process and measurement of emotional strength. Jin Li,[6] professor at Brown University, supports Stigler's view but takes a step back to think about how different cultures view the origins of academic excellence in order to explain these contrasting approaches to failure and struggle. She compares the widely held Western belief that intelligence is what you were born with and hence who you are – smart or not – with the widely held Asian belief that intelligence comes from what you do and how you deal with struggle and failure is part of that. Hence, struggle is built into the learning process, specifically to build intelligence.

---

5   Dr James W. Stigler is Professor of Psychology at UCLA. He is co-author of *The Teaching Gap* (with James Hiebert, Free Press, 1999) and *The Learning Gap* (with Harold Stevenson, Simon & Schuster, 1992)

6   Dr Jin Li is Professor of Education and Human Development at Brown University where her research focuses on learning models, children's learning beliefs and their socialisation across different cultures and ethnic groups. For more information, see vivo.brown.edu/display/jili

If we teach our children, implicitly or explicitly, that struggle indicates a lack of ability it will affect how they approach failure. On the other hand, if struggle indicates strength, then our children are more likely to engage with it and go the distance. This includes all manner of disappointments and failed lemonade stands.

Singapore-based education researcher and professor, Manu Kapur,[7] argues that if failure is such a powerful teacher, why wait for it to happen to you? Why not intentionally create situations where students can learn by failing? This seemingly unorthodox method, coined *productive failure*, is gaining an audience the world over as it sits in the corner opposite the traditional mode of teaching – direct instruction. We all know the latter method – teach a theory or process and then allow students to implement in practice what they have just learned in theory. We also know that this lacks two essential elements of long-term learning: curiosity and challenge.

Using a productive failure approach, students are given a problem that they don't know and can't find the answer to, and then allowed to work on it for some time, conceptualising and trying different solutions that may or may not work. This promotes curiosity about both the problem and its solution. The idea is not necessarily for them to solve it but draw on prior knowledge, and each other, to understand what they are dealing with. Sounds like real life, doesn't it?

From his research Prof Kapur has shown that presenting problems back to front like this results in deeper and more flexible learning. He argues that integrating new and old knowledge, while grappling with a challenge, leads to a much deeper understanding

---

7   Dr Manu Kapur is an Associate Professor in the Curriculum, Teaching and Learning Academic Group and a researcher at the Learning Sciences Lab at the National Institute of Education of Singapore. For more on Productive Failure see his website at www.manukapur. com and his upcoming book *Productive Failure*, Springer.

of the issues as well as the final solution. Of course, it also creates curiosity about what the actual solution is. Think about it, if you've been working on a problem that you couldn't solve, wouldn't you want to know the answer? Above all, it encourages sustained thought and the ability to work on something even though there may not be a feel-good reward waiting at the end.

If you're still not convinced that a little failure goes a long way then Astro Teller, Google's "Captain of Moonshots" and the grandson of the theoretical physicist Edward Teller will remind you that, "Being afraid to fail is a glass ceiling on the level of success that can be achieved." And he should know, because failing several times over on the same project is considered a key ingredient in Google's success and hence, creating a culture of successful failure is top of his agenda.

So next time your son is struggling to set up the tent under the stars for your night out camping, try not to rush in and help him out. Give him only a few pointers and be ready to answer his questions. Or when your daughter has just been booted off the selection for the *We've Got Talent* competition, help her work through the steps leading up to the "failure" and look for the leverage points where she could have done something different or come to a different conclusion about her talents.

> I have not failed. I've just found 10,000 ways that won't work.
>
> ~ **Thomas A. Edison**

9.3

HOW TO BE AN INVENTOR

Our modern lifestyle is not a political creation. Before 1700, everybody was poor as hell. Life was short and brutish. But then we started inventing – electricity, steam engines, microprocessors, understanding genetics and medicine and things like that. Yes, stability and education are important – I'm not taking anything away from that – but innovation is the real driver of progress.

~ **Bill Gates,** *Rolling Stone,* **March 2014**

In the spirit of productive failure, I challenge you to invent a method of innovation that could give your child a structured approach to creating something new – to be an inventor. Jot down your initial thoughts here before moving on.

Now don't be shy, write down what you're thinking. No one has to know, my lips are sealed.

_____

_____

_____

_____

_____

_____

Let's have a look at your method.

I imagine it started in the neighbourhood of identifying a problem, then it may have sat down at the table of brainstorming solutions or even stepped out to gather information and data. It most likely ended in the prototyping lab where each new iteration inched it closer to a global patent. Did I guess correctly – at least for some of the steps?

Most models of _innovation_ that our children are exposed to include similar steps. As you can imagine, the more inherently curious and creative children will excel at this, so will the extroverts and more popular girls and boys. The process of actually finding that initial good idea, that spark of genius, is traditionally ensconced in the brainstorming section. This is not a process that takes a child, or anyone, by the hand and says, "This is how you think up something new." Rather it says, "Go on then, just come up with something, anything, no matter how crazy it might be. Think BIG." When you're in middle school and you haven't had much exposure to new ideas and technologies, then just thinking big is a pretty daunting task.

It is for most adults I work with. I find that many of them have had their biggest ideas deflated through company politics, rejection or an overbearing boss. During a systems thinking session at a large bank in Asia, I met a young chap who was not only charming, smart and quick on the mental draw but also a tremendous team player. A natural leader who knew when to lead his team from the front or herd more shy participants from the side. It was clear he was popular and on a fast track into a senior management position. When it came time to solve the final and largest challenge in the programme, he excused himself from his team, sat outside in the elevator lobby and worked away at a solution alone. Of course I was curious about his behaviour but equally curious to see what he would produce. Was it arrogance that led him to the lobby or a mistrust of his team's ability? Everyone took offence.

Unsurprisingly, his solution was tremendous, unlike any I had seen before or since. I actually wasn't sure if it was "right" simply because I didn't know enough to evaluate it. I asked him afterwards why he had chosen to work alone and not share his idea with the group that he had unofficially coached and led for two full days.

If I may paraphrase his answer from memory, it went like this, "Well, my solution was either going to be really good, or really bad, either way it's so different it would be seen as extreme – an outlier. Something so uncomfortable and risky that the whole team would never buy into – they're a pretty conservative bunch of analysts and economists – no offence! I would've had to compromise on many fronts and my idea would have been reduced to an average fix that everybody could feel comfortable with."

In my corporate work, I spend a tremendous amount of time

undoing the damage wrecked by the status quo. A particularly pervasive norm is our unquestioned tradition of running every problem through a brainstorming session. Brainstorming is an interesting social experiment but, as far as problem solving goes, it remains a blunt instrument, especially in groups peppered with mixed abilities or confidence levels. It's a well-documented blunt instrument with decades of research telling us to avoid it like the MSG in Chinese takeaways. With the increased focus on teamwork at schools, brainstorming is, unfortunately, still the main tool used to undertake problem solving. I'd love to rant on and toss the research about but I'll resist rehashing what others have already said and merely reiterate that brainstorming is not the way to go. But if I remove brainstorming from your child's innovation process, then there's a gaping hole in it, isn't there?

Of course there are several enhanced brainstorming processes that improve its hit rate and reduce the effects of groupthink. IDEO's popular Design Thinking process is one such candidate. I taught it for many years and was always amazed at the crazy but useful stuff my students could come up in the "solutions" part of the creative-thinking process. But even an improved brainstorming exercise doesn't provide the genesis of a great idea, something that, till now, we've left up to some idiosyncratic talent that can't be quantified or serialised.

Perhaps it's true that the method of innovation is the greatest invention of all. So I went looking for the inscrutable idea behind an idea and I found it between the covers of corporate literature in a process that has come to light thanks to the meeting of two diverse minds.

Jacob Goldenberg and Drew Boyd are the co-authors of *Inside The Box*,[1] a resource promising "a proven system of creativity for breakthrough results". Their system is delivering on that promise so well it can now be read in 13 languages around the world. Through extensive research and their own experience across the corporate and academic sectors, Jacob and Drew show that any one of us can innovate using what we already know and have access to. They call their process Systemic Inventive Thinking or SIT. It proved so user friendly to adults that Drew wondered if children would be able to innovate using the principles of SIT, too.

While Drew has a deep corporate pedigree, his co-author, Jacob, leads their research at the Interdisciplinary Centre in Herzliya, Israel and as a visiting professor at Columbia University. I had the opportunity of chatting with Drew from the University of Cincinnati, Ohio, where he is the executive director of the Master of Science in Marketing Program and Assistant Professor of Marketing and Innovation. In his 17 years with Johnson & Johnson before that, Drew founded their Marketing Mastery Program, an internal "marketing university" benchmarked by companies such as General Electric, Procter & Gamble, Kraft, and Merck. One of the things they taught employees there was how to systematically invent new medical products and integrate these inventions into long-range strategic plans. You read that right: they *taught* them how to innovate. Drew believes anyone can innovate with the right system and encouragement, including children.

"The corporate world," he says, "is very good at adopting new methods to generate increased revenue for shareholders.

1   Boyd, D. & Goldenberg, J. (2013) *Inside the Box*. New York: Simon and Schuster
    See also: www.insidetheboxinnovation.com

Schools, however, don't have the same motivation to do this. It's expensive to adopt new subject matter and technologies. They certainly recognise the need for creativity, but they aren't really sure how to implement it." Drew offered to teach an innovation programme, How To Be An Inventor, at his son's school. His offer was rejected initially as the administrator felt "it would set too high an expectation of their children because creativity cannot be taught – to anyone".

Drew persisted and when his offer was finally accepted, it proved so popular with mainstream school children that he expanded it to work with special-needs children, "who," he adds, "innovate just as capably as everyone else once they are taught how."

"In the future we will all need to become better at solving problems," he explains. "Everyday problems, personal as well as corporate problems. Almost every area of society will face global challenges – our children will have to innovate in order to be successful and those that know how will be better at it."

Through their desire to spread word of their method to as many parents, teachers and carers as possible, Drew gave me permission to share the basic steps of it with you. This will get you started but I urge you to visit their website at www.insidetheboxinnovation.com. There you will find a generous array of free resources for both corporates, parents and teachers – PowerPoint slides, course syllabi and loads of other fun stuff to support and add depth and colour to your own efforts.

I bet you're ready to hear about that method of innovation now?

Subtracting Without Detracting

In the SIT method, subtraction is the process of eliminating an essential component of a system to create something new or at the very least reframe the problem at hand. Hang on, why would we do that? Well, an iPhone without a phone is an iPod, a travel agent without an actual agent is online booking, a book without pages is an ebook. See where this is going? Subtraction is a powerful and popular method of creative innovation that isn't that hard to do with an open mind and a touch of mental bravery. Drew and Jacob advise that we write down all essential components of the system or problem we are working with and eliminate each of them one-by-one to re-imagine the system. Then, ask who would use such a thing and why.

Let's re-imagine our lemonade stand from the previous chapter using subtraction.

An inventory of essential components would include: lemonade, cups, a table, a cashbox, a sales person, customers and a sunny day in the park. Let's begin by subtracting the lemonade. Well, that wouldn't work too well, because then we wouldn't have a lemonade stand at all. So let's leave that well enough alone and move on to the cups. Could I subtract the cups? Of course, but how would we serve our lemonade? My son's solution was little plastic bags with a straw in them, tied with twine that seals the bag closed around the straw and then loops to form a little handle.

Lemonade that you can't put down!

Who would want this? Kids on bicycles or skateboards in the park or cycling home from school on a hot day with empty juice bottles. They can hang these little juice packets on their handlebars and sip as they zip along. Living in Asia, this wasn't a far stretch of the imagination at all as this is exactly how local drink stalls sell their drinks to go – in bags with straws that won't ever spill as you commute. Yet this market has never been tapped for kids, or in the West.

OK, what's next? How about the table? If we don't have cups, do we need a table? No, we can bring a clothes rail or hang our pre-filled bags of lemonade on the branches of the cotton tree in the centre of the park. Wouldn't that attract attention? We could probably either eliminate or substitute each of the essential components in our lemonade stand with something that we have readily to hand.

Using only what we already have access to is an important principle of the SIT method, named the Closed World Principle. The best and fastest way to innovate is to look at what is readily available in our environment. We all know the feeling of coming across a genius or nifty solution that seems so simple yet had eluded us until the moment we saw someone else create it for the first time.

Those things that are available to your child right now, the things that you generally don't give a second thought to as you sail through your day, are the things that can be used as raw materials in your child's innovation efforts. Do you usually have to go out and buy specialist bits and nifty bobs every time your child needs an interesting costume for book character day or a quirky contraption for the science fair? With this method you may not need to at all.

Research in this area is plentiful and conclusions agree that

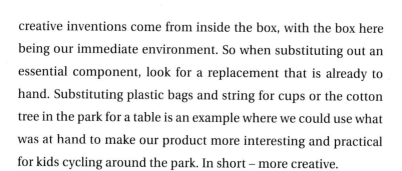

creative inventions come from inside the box, with the box here being our immediate environment. So when substituting out an essential component, look for a replacement that is already to hand. Substituting plastic bags and string for cups or the cotton tree in the park for a table is an example where we could use what was at hand to make our product more interesting and practical for kids cycling around the park. In short – more creative.

TIPS AND TAKEAWAYS FROM CHAPTER 9

1. Research shows that we are born creative and learn to be uncreative as we age.

2. Understanding that failure is a rich source of data and being able to extract that data from failures will set your children up to fail well and withstand the blows that inevitably come bundled with the innovation process.

3. Innovation requires the ability to create something new and useful – often from existing materials and ideas. Creativity certainly helps this process along but a lack of creative smarts isn't a deal breaker as far as innovation goes.

4. Innovation is a process and can be taught using a method of innovation such as Systemic Inventive Thinking or IDEO's Design Thinking.

OVER TO YOU

In classical Athens, *paideia*[1] was the name given to the process of cultivation of the person towards civic virtue.[2] This was achieved through intellectual, moral and physical refinement with a programme of rhetoric, grammar, arithmetic and medicine as well as training in gymnastics and wrestling, completed by moral education through the study of music, poetry and philosophy. All these subjects where believed to nurture refined and worthy citizens. Facilitated by the aristocracy, *paideia* was not available to manual labourers or women, only free men who had free time or *schole* to invest in the pursuit of reason. It was only later, during the enlightenment,[3] that education became a means to achieve freedom rather than confined to those who were already free.

In opposition to *paideia*, education in the Greek city-state of Sparta was designed to serve the military, creating obedient, courageous and strong warriors through lessons in sports,

---

1 A system of education implemented in the 5th and 6th century BC in the Greek City State of Athens.
2 Civic virtue is the cultivation of habits of personal living that are claimed to be important for the success of the community. Civic virtue is also the dedication of citizens to the common welfare of their community even at the cost of their individual interests. The identification of the character traits that constitute civic virtue has been a major concern of political philosophy. – Wikipedia
3 A European intellectual movement of the late 17th and 18th centuries emphasising reason and individualism rather than tradition.

endurance and fighting. A subservient, loyal and illiterate population resulted.

Free from Western influences, China's earliest education ideals[4] were to produce a small group of literati that could govern the country. This group would rise through a series of examinations, which were open to anyone and held the rare[5] promise of becoming a scholar-official at the pinnacle of Chinese society. Such an achievement confirmed that you were expertly versed in the philosophical and ethical, socio-political teachings of the Confucian classics and therefore fit to govern over others. After 1,000 years of dominance, this civil service examination was abolished in 1905 because China was changing. The last years of the Qing Dynasty and early years of the Republic required a patriotic, hardworking and united citizenry and the education system was the tool to create it.

Throughout time, education existed to serve a specific goal or uphold an ideal for a specific group of stakeholders. But where are we today? Should education be a tool to cultivate good citizens that can maintain a base level of intelligence and skill within a particular society, or is it to help an individual achieve excellence in their own life, to unlock their idiosyncratic potentials and succeed in their chosen pursuits? Maybe it's to further the corporate agenda and secure economic growth for the country that invests in educating its citizens? Education is a public good, after all. Are governments, industries or parents responsible for making this decision unilaterally or collectively? Who are the architects of the education system in your country and who do they serve?

---

4   Chi-hou Chan, MA, (2006). *Historical and Cultural Background of Education in China*.
5   Less than 2% of those who sat the highest level exam passed.

An alternative raison d'être for the existence of education is that it is responsible for the cultivation of humanity, of global citizens capable of transcending individual differences to form a cohesive and productive global community.

Recent thinking about the aims of education has gone disturbingly awry both in the United States and abroad. Anxiously focused on national economic growth, we increasingly treat education as though its primary goal were to teach students to be economically productive rather than to think critically and become knowledgeable and empathetic citizens. This short-sighted focus on profitable skills has eroded our ability to criticise authority, reduced our sympathy with the marginalised and different, and damaged our competence to deal with complex global problems. And the loss of these basic capacities jeopardises the health of democracies and the hope of a decent world.[6]

~ **Martha Craven Nussbaum,**
Not for Profit: Why Democracy Needs the Humanities

---

6   Martha Craven Nussbaum is an American philosopher and the current Ernst Freund Distinguished Service Professor of Law and Ethics at the University of Chicago.

I write this in the wake of the UK's vote to exit the European union and the aftermath of xenophobia, regret, fear and uncertainty that has engulfed this country, and the world, in the space of a few short days. Right now, the utopian ideal of a global citizen seems very far away until I remind myself of just how far we have come as a species from the days of empires and authoritarian rulers. I disagree with the severity of Professor Nussbaum's sentiment. I think there *is* hope – and the hope lies with parents, teachers, headmasters and caregivers who want more for their children and their world.

Never before have citizens of democracies had more power to create their own narratives and change the course of history. Over 30 million individuals voted in the referendum to exit the European union. They were informed of the consequences of such a vote and then handed the responsibility of decision – an enormous responsibility. Imagine if every voter had learnt sound decision making at school? How to separate rhetoric from facts, think about frames and motives, identify stereotypes and thinking mistakes, think empathetically and make non-emotive decisions?

The role and purpose of education is being debated by stakeholders around the world, including governments, educators and industry leaders. It's an important question at a pivotal moment of change and flux in the system – although I fear the most underrepresented voice is that of the parent.

I remember choosing to be a parent. My husband and I actually sat down and discussed it. As we are both economists, we looked at the financial implications of having and raising a child and agreed that, financially, it made no sense at all. Then we forgot about all that nonsense and fell pregnant anyway. We simply wanted to be parents. Throughout this journey, I have asked myself: What is the purpose of being a parent? Why are we gifted with babies who know nothing of the world, who need guidance, love, protection and then the ability and freedom to leave us and repeat the cycle of life on their own?

Why Are *You* a Parent?

I didn't become a parent to change the world but now that I am, I understand the role that I have to play in creating a brighter future for it. You see, the most influence I have is not as a lecturer, a coach or an author, but as a mother. I have the ability to shape the thoughts, personality and behaviours of one precious life. A boy who trusts me unconditionally and believes everything I tell him (for now). He is my hope for this world. If every one of us could raise our children as thinkers and good decision makers, the world *will* be a better place, and we would have played our parts.

It's over to you now at mission control. Go! Save the world, raise a thinker!

Unless someone like you cares a whole awful lot, nothing is going to get better. It's not.

~ **Dr Seuss**

ABOUT THE AUTHOR

Tremaine has lived and worked in Asia, Africa and Europe, coaching and lecturing in leadership, behavioural finance, decision science and critical thinking to multinational organisations, government agencies and on MBA and undergraduate programmes. Whilst in Singapore she designed and facilitated a Critical Thinking training programme for the Monetary Authority/Central Bank of Singapore and other government agencies.

She has a BCom in Information Systems, an MSc in Financial Economics, is a certified executive coach, *Huffington Post* blogger and the author and co-author of several books. She lives with her husband, son, spaniel and books, between her head, Singapore and London. She currently travels from London.

Tremaine is founding director of The Coaching Club – offering executive coaching via subscription to organisations serious about maintaining a coaching culture to drive engagement, performance and happiness.

To find out more, visit www.tremainedupreez.com and www.coachingclub.co.uk. For more resources on raising thinkers and regular webinars, visit www.raisingthinkersbook.co